Shaking the Foundations

Tadao Ando · Hiroshi Hara · Itsuko Hasegawa · Osamu Ishiyam
Arata Isozaki · Toyo Ito · Atsushi Kitagawara · Kengo Kum
Kisho Kurokawa · Fumihiko Maki · Hiroshi Naito · Kazu
Shinohara · Ryoji Suzuki · Riken Yamamoto · Hajime Yatsuk

Shaking the Foundations

Japanese Architects
in Dialogue

Edited by Christopher Knabe and Joerg Rainer Noennig

Foreword by David B. Stewart
Introduction by Wilhelm Klauser

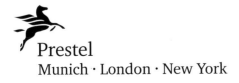

Prestel
Munich · London · New York

© Copyright 1999 Prestel Verlag
Munich – London – New York

Die Deutsche Bibliothek – CIP-Einheitsaufnahme
Shaking the foundations : Japanese architects in dialogue / ed. by Christopher Knabe
and Joerg Rainer Noennig. Foreword by David B. Stewart. Introd. by Wilhelm Klauser.
- Munich ; London ; New York : Prestel, 1999
ISBN 3-7913-2000-9

Library of Congress Cataloging-in-Publication Data is available.

Front cover: Kounji Buddhist Temple, Tokyo, 1991.
Back cover, from left to right: Hasegawa, Sumida Culture Factory; Kurokawa, Shirase
Polar Expedition Museum; Kitagawara, Scala Building; Kuma, Water/Glass Villa.
Photographic acknowledgments on p. 160.

Prestel-Verlag
Mandlstraße 26
D-80802 Munich, Germany
Tel.: (89) 38-17-09-0
Fax: (89) 38-17-09-35

4 Bloomsbury Place
London, WC1A 2QA
Tel.: (171) 323 5004
Fax: (171) 636 8004

16 West 22 Street
New York, NY 10010
Tel.: (212) 627-8199
Fax: (212) 627-9866

Prestel books are available worldwide. Please contact your nearest bookseller or any of
the above addresses for information concerning your local distributor.

Copy-edited by Jayne Louise Rollinson
Designed by Daniela Petrini
Lithography by reproteam siefert, Ulm/Böfingen, Germany
Printed and bound by Bosch Druck, Landshut, Germany

Printed in Germany on acid-free paper

ISBN 3-7913-2000-9

Contents

Foreword

by David B. Stewart

As one of the architects interviewed in this book forthrightly says, middle- and high-brow Japanese architectural culture since World War II has evolved into "essentially the science of consciousness and the science of the body." In this recent flight, architects have almost certainly taken their cue from the medieval cult of tea, which from about the time of the Western Renaissance represented an escape from the violence and hierarchy of a militaristic and feudal society and which attempted to expand the horizons of the individual—albeit within the framework of a familiar religious and aesthetic tradition. This is all the more to be wondered at, since the majority of Japanese believe architecture to be the science of construction, a mere facet of engineering, a fact referred to more than once in the pages which follow.

In my book *The Making of a Modern Japanese Architecture: 1868 to the Present* I attempted to show how this came about in broad social and political terms since the so-called Meiji Restoration when Japan became a modern nation. Two bearers of this complex transformation, Kazuo Shinohara and Arata Isozaki, are preeminent in rather different ways, and both are given an opportunity to speak by Christopher Knabe and Joerg Rainer Noennig.

In a way unprecedented in the history of architecture outside the Florentine Renaissance, aesthetics here take pride of place in notions of architecture, or, as Kengo Kuma notes of the tea ethic and its modern-day avatar, "gardening, lifestyle, and architecture are not to be separated but are rather to be conceived as an entire world." Or, perhaps a better analogy is the English eighteenth century, another epoch of the connoisseur and of "total" art, nearer to us both in time and in terms of modern, notably societal concerns.

Yet, despite the occasionally somewhat idealistic remarks that surface in the following dialogues, even this is not the whole story. (For one thing, gardening is a totally discredited activity in Japan, relegated today to the artisan corps of professional gardeners.) It is nonetheless of interest that many of the techniques believed to underpin traditional aesthetics, and hence architecture, have been preserved and transmitted via the tenets of dry landscaping where few if any living plant material is used.

What comes across strongly in the following pages is a continued flight from reality to metaphor. It has often been said that for the generation of Japanese architects already active or beginning their work in the 1960s—five of whom, Hiroshi Hara, Arata Isozaki, Fumihiko Maki, Kisho Kurokawa, and Kazuo Shinohara have a part in the present dialogues—metaphor looks, to the Western eye, like Formalism. Nevertheless, owing to the sheer density of habitat in much of Asia and the price of land in places such as Hong Kong and Tokyo, as well as the ephemeral nature of building referred to again and again by the Japanese architects in this volume, many buildings constructed since the war were conceived of, so to speak, as place-markers, or exemplars of theory, as their architects clearly state.

By the 1970s, and certainly from the 1980s on (the period with which this book is principally concerned), a transition to a Realism of sorts had taken place, as Riken Yamamoto notes in his interview. However, Japanese society remains rigid, not to say ossified and sclerotic, as the economy and its political back-up—or lack of it—demonstrates. Part of what Postmodernism has shown, in the West, and notably in America, is that interest in architecture is often a stand-in for what people otherwise do not have. Why should things be different in Japan? All the same, dissatisfaction runs deeper here in terms of a sort of socio-ethnological conformism, proving the old shibboleth that the nail that stands out gets hit down.

Thus, also, the stakes have changed. Before World War II Modernism in Japan, as elsewhere, was viewed as a vehicle of renewal with a helping hand from technology. When, in wartime, the modernist style was officially suppressed, a radical traditionalism of sorts emerged, almost imperceptibly, as an antidote to the enforced return to "traditional" values. By 1960 when Metabolism hove into view, it was largely as a retrograde compromise struck with the conservative democratic resurgence. But the ideological compliance with the strictures of a "mass society" that was indeed new was publicized as representing the new social mobility of the postwar era. Demographic mobility was directed towards Japan's cities, while the power-base remained unreconstructedly rural, not to say indulgent, benighted, and corrupt.

The architecture of the later 1960s and the early 1970s remained that of an identifiable "counterculture", one that now at the end of the century is in the final stages of internalization. For a number of reasons, Japan has over the past decades subsidized a stupefying program of public works, echoing but vastly surpassing those of the Meiji era of 1868–1912. Initially these overwhelmingly concerned transport infrastructures; however more recently amenity programs have been added, including social service infrastructures, museums, cultural centers, and townscape refurbishing, with various national and local authorities reaching out toward

independent architects, who have grown up and been educated under the aegis of the "counterculture". These are the somewhat confused and bewildered voices of the majority in the following pages, some taking what they can get, others querying their own "avant-garde" or "countercultural" status, yet others willing to look for a way out that is probably non-existent.

However, the make-over of a counterculture into a normative vehicle is hardly a fate unique to Japan, although the hullabaloo in recent years over the perceived value of public, and particularly state, commissions gives pause for thought. At the high end of the scale, there is still a deal of good work although little enough is breathtaking. Construction standards continue to provoke admiration abroad, especially in terms of the mastery of concrete, however maintenance provisions are too often non-existent, while standards of architectural photography are consummate.

Finally, the most interesting aspect of these interviews is their divergences of opinion, when they do occur. To choose not altogether at random among two architects who are exact contemporaries, I note Toyo Ito's championship of "mentally light architecture" in the sense of buildings that "can easily be rethought." Consider this, against the stated importance given to "creating architecture that continues to live on in your mind after you have left the building" from Tadao Ando, Tokyo University's newly minted Professor of Architecture. Foundations are indeed shaking; but no single trend predominates.

Introduction
Rules and Identities

by Wilhelm Klauser

"The mechanism of Japanese behavior resembles the playing of a game. Principles are not an issue. All that matters are the rules. The ultimate pleasure is to respect, to follow and become absorbed in those rules. Once the game becomes established, it is made even more complicated, refined and finally becomes an obsession."[1]

1.

In September 1959, the journal *Shinkenchiku* featured an apartment block that had been built on reclaimed land in the Bay of Tokyo. A rumor that had been going around in architectural circles was suddenly confirmed: Kunio Maekawa, who had worked with Le Corbusier in Paris during a stay in Europe before the war and who, as a teacher, had influenced a whole generation of Japanese architects and had played a major role in adapting the Modern Movement, the International Style, to circumstances in Japan, had created a structure of hitherto unknown radicalness. He had designed a 10-story, rigid concrete skeleton frame with a "skip-floor" construction. Laid out in a pragmatic manner within this framework were a large number of identical, tiny apartments, all finished exclusively in Japanese style. The care Maekawa devoted to the design of the external spaces and the semi-public access routes to the apartment block was exemplary. Here, the qualities of the historical Japanese city center, the legendary *shita-machi*, with its finely differentiated gradation from private to public realms, were developed from a planar form into the third dimension. Disturbingly, though, the building had been erected on newly won land in the middle of an area of water, where no building had ever stood before. In addition to the provocative act of turning its back on the native soil of Japan, the building thrust itself up on powerful, expressively shaped concrete piers. In its juxtaposition of hitherto irreconcilable opposites, it represented a completely new approach. Clearly contrasted with Japanese architecture that had hitherto taken its bearings mainly from Europe and, after the war, from America, too, this new structure also broke with the principles underlying traditional forms of Japanese construction. For the first time, an independent Japanese version of Modernism began to manifest itself. It was a final leavetaking from the neo-colonialism[2] that had dominated Japanese architecture up to that time. The building was a response to an unmistakably Japanese situation and presented a most convincing solution. The Harumi apartment complex translated the dimensions of the new cities that had developed with breathtaking speed in postwar Japan into a satisfying image. Confronted with this building, critics were rendered speechless not by the principle of a multi-story structure, not by the quality of the external spaces, nor indeed by an act of repetition that verged on the obsessive. It was the fact that the main influence on the West was no longer the modest Japanese tradition of craft skills, but a modern Japanese version of Western architecture; and this was exerting not a marginal, but a key influence on the major centers of the world.[3] Like some menacing, over-dimensioned battleship, an alien building seemed to be approaching the city, providing some idea of the future toward which society was moving.

The development received an enthusiastic response. The massive nature of the structure—in contrast to which the delicate quality of the Japanese living room is brought out all the more distinctly—excited not only the adherents of Brutalism; for the unexpected sensitivity in the treatment of the interior spaces relativized the structural dimensions. One of the illustrations published in *Shinkenchiku* shows an idyllic, Japanese interior from which the view extends out over the massive concrete balcony balustrade to an industrial landscape of dredging boats and factory chimneys silhouetted against the horizon. Set in a reinforced concrete framework—in an "international" material and an "international" system—a certain way of life here asserted its continued right to existence, in spite of the changes that had taken place in its surroundings. For the first time, this housing development openly revealed an unexpected duality: a disturbing reciprocity of constriction and space, regionalism and internationalism, past and future, which is a recurrent phenomenon in Japanese architecture of the 20th century. Since the creation of this building, efforts to resolve this dichotomy, to reconcile the polarities, have had a formative influence on Japanese architecture and indeed on its reception abroad.

2.

At the beginning of the 1960s, the standard of living in Japan had finally reached the level of before the war. The country found itself involved in an unprecedented economic race to make up lost ground and catch up with the Western industrial nations. The role of architects in this situation was to propose a valid form for a society that was opening itself increasingly to external influences. The architects sought "a universal concept and method which would be completely Japanese in its conception but which would also be applicable internationally,"[4] as the architectural critic Noboru Kawazoe remarked. Kawazoe was one of the mentors and founders of the Metabolist movement. The World Design Conference held in Tokyo in 1960 at last provided an opportunity to present a specifically Japanese form of design[5] that had taken the Werkbund as its model.

The Metabolists, who made their first public appearance at that time, presented their theories at the conference. Their view of architecture was no longer dominated by the machine image that had inspired the Modern Movement, but by a biological one; in other words, in their architecture, they sought analogies with living organisms.[6]

In their architectural concept, therefore, the Metabolists initially returned to a specifically Japanese theme, reviving the idea of the "floating world" that may be found in the history of that country: in a civilization that had blossomed 200 years earlier in the urban culture of Edo and that was characterized by a constant process of change and its aestheticization. On the other hand, the new approach took account in a much more pragmatic way of the uninhibited expansion that had transformed the metropolis of Tokyo after the war into an enormous conurbation in which 30 million people lived. A new habitat had evolved, and a completely different strategy was needed to come to terms with its dynamics. All this was reflected in the different approach adopted by architects.

The project to build over Tokyo Bay exceeded all known dimensions. In 1960, Kenzo Tange presented plans for a new city that was meant to provide living space for 10 million people. He proposed a bridge-like linear city over 11 miles long that would span the bay in a chain of large-scale, multi-story transport loops. Located within these loops was the center of the city, which comprised a number of high towers raised above the ground. Extending irregularly from both sides of the primary transport and infrastructure spine were strips that were subdivided into ever smaller segments. Attached to these strips were large A-section frame structures, which, Tange proposed, were to contain the residential functions. Every element of this city was a megastructure in its own right, a framework into which the constantly changing needs of the inhabitants could be plugged. It provided a basis for unlimited growth.

Even more staggering than the heroic dimensions of this scheme was the degree to which it was elaborated. "The scale is unnerving; so is the formal control over all the parts of the professedly aformal and uncontrollable megaform...."[7]

The project reveals the differences that existed between the work of the Metabolists and contemporary developments in France and Italy. It was no longer clear whether the Japanese projects were visionary urban Utopias or could actually be built. Never before and never again since has a megastructure on an urban scale seemed so tangibly close to realization as this. A new society was assuming form under the guiding hand of architecture, the critics exulted: "Tange begins with the problems of today and proceeds to the problems of tomorrow, attempting to solve them by means of constantly evolving technology. This step-by-step extrapolation of the ideas of today into the future is clearly distinguished from the sheer sensationalism that often masquerades as Utopia."[8]

It was indeed technology—and directly associated with it, industry—that lent these projects a convincing quality of realism and which subsequently and with increasing clarity became the motive force behind the architecture of the Metabolists.

As a result of population movements within Japan, the Metabolists calculated that 1.3 million new dwelling units a year were needed in the major cities. It was clear that this goal could be achieved only through an unremitting program of industrialization of the means of construction. From 1961, Kisho Kurokawa, Kuniyori Kikutake, and Masao Otaka, the founder members of the Metabolist movement, were architectural advisers to the Nippon Prefabrication Co., a consortium of leading construction firms whose goal it was to respond to these developments.

Initially, these activities seemed to be an idealistic attempt on the part of architects to relieve the pressures caused by rigid land divisions and irreversible property ownership structures in cities—by escaping to artificial plateaux, into the air or underground—in order to provide the inhabitants with a new and specifically Japanese habitat that would reflect the true circumstances of their lives. Within a few years, however, these measures were turned into a vehicle for industry. Ideas of an ongoing, dynamic process of change which seemed inevitable at that time, were entirely in accordance with these aims. Metabolism was conceivable only as a process of growth, a process of constant expansion, the goal of which was the continuous extension of what already existed.

3.

As early as 1962, in his "Future City" collage, Arata Isozaki had drawn attention to the one-sided orientation of the movement. He showed a Metabolist city rising above a field of ancient ruins. The colossal piers of a load-bearing structure were developed directly from the bases of crumbling Doric columns beneath. Here, for the first time in Metabolist architecture, a possible end of the futuristic plans was indicated, an end that promised to be no different from that of the former city from which the new one had risen. It proved impossible to sustain the promise of eternal youth and the strength and sense of blitheness implicit to the perpetual process of Metabolist renewal. Nevertheless, nearly eight years were to pass before this became apparent.

In 1970, the World Exposition was staged in Osaka. The Metabolist architects, by that time guarantors of all that was technically and architecturally superlative, wished to create a space of the utmost flexibility for this event. It was to represent an ideal image of the future city. The centerpiece of the exhibition was a huge roof structure, beneath which the peoples of the world were to gather and participate in a peaceful cultural exchange. This structure was to be a final reflection of the Metabolists' idealistic concepts; for the public proved to be more or less indifferent to the design. The sole focus of attention was the entertainment program on offer within this setting. The World Exposition had transformed itself into a gigantic pleasure machine that left no room for noble ideas. It was not the architecture that afforded a glimpse of the city of the future, but the overwhelming commercial success of this undertaking. In Montreal three years earlier, the coming together of people from all over the world had been an event to celebrate. Now, in Osaka, three-dimensional advertising structures erected for industrial concerns were set alongside the national pavilions, overwhelming them from almost every point of view. In almost all cases, the design of these structures was quite unrelated to the industry they represented. Their purpose, it seemed, was simply to lend industry a progressive image – an image that in practice was less a vision of the architecture of the future than an amateurish depiction of it.[9] In the end, the lasting impression of the exposition was that of the huge masses of people. They moved about quite naturally in enormous, futuristic stage sets, in a Potemkin village, the architecture of which conjured the vision of a future that, in this form, had long been redundant.

Although classical modernism had been the source of inspiration for the new Japanese architecture and had helped to raise it to a consistently high level of achievement, the social relevance of the work of those architects who had taken it as their model was systematically eroded. By succumbing to the embrace of industry and politics, architecture lost its independence and strength and was transformed into an object of social fantasy. Because of their allegiance to the avant-garde – not in spite of it – most progressive architects received the blessing of society to determine its social behavior. The architectural expression of the avant-garde was recognized without much opposition. As a result, most avant-garde architects were overtaken by the revolutionary forms they themselves had helped create,[10] and architecture transformed itself into a caricature. In a strangely perverse way, it seemed that precisely where capitalism was developing in its most brazen form, the claims advanced in the political debate of 1968 – a radical debate in Japan, too – were being met. The masses took possession of the new city. In this respect, architecture neither reflected the existing balance of power, nor was it able to assume a critical distance. It simply declined to a *quantité négligeable*.

4.

In Osaka, the heroic phase of Japanese modern architecture petered out in two directions. On the one hand, its unsuccessful attempts to give the new society an appropriate form had become patently evident. The "end of the great stories", the *grands récits*, as J.-F. Lyotard expressed it, was in sight. The systematic Marxist or Hegelian interpretation of the world was subjected to doubt. The massive, permanent architectural designs no longer corresponded to the developments taking place in society, even if these designs pursued the ideals of change and flexibility. The mercury-poisoning catastrophe that occurred in Minamata, where chemical plants had been pouring untreated waste into the sea for decades, destroying the balance of nature, made people aware for the first time of the hitherto unsuspected environmental destruction that had accompanied the rapid economic growth of the country. The sense of affinity with nature that Japanese society had always taken for granted and on which the Metabolist architects had based their theory, had ceased to exist. Even at the World Exposition in Osaka, an attempt had been made to set the site off against its unpleasant surroundings by transforming it into an artificial hilly landscape. The argument of economic growth and its perpetual continuation, which might have been used to justify the irreversible damage it had caused, suddenly seemed open to doubt. Heavy industry, which had hitherto been a motor of the economy, declined in importance with the rise of other competitors in Asia; and suddenly, the central roof of the World Exposition, a gigantic space-frame structure that had elicited the praise of Western critics for its dimensions and its concept of uniting the peoples of the world, seemed strangely dated in the eyes of Japanese architects, since its form had evidently been inspired by those very chemical plants, refineries, and shipping lines whose significance was now rapidly declining. The oil crises painfully reminded the Japanese of the vulnerability of their country: Japan was suddenly in the throes of a recession.

The ensuing decade was marked by a process of economic restructuring. In his election program in 1972, Kakuei Tanaka, who became prime minister of the country, proposed the reconstruction of the entire Japanese archipelago. It was a project that, despite the new and widespread suspicion of technocracy, reflected the general mood of crisis—a crisis that this fundamental act of reorganization and the construction measures accompanying it were meant to overcome. The project was implemented only in outline, but its sweeping nature had a lasting negative influence on all subsequent large-scale restructuring plans.

The economic crisis was only the first obvious token of a development that was directly reflected in the volume of architectural commissions. Something that the World Exposition and the many subsequent large-scale construction schemes had impressed upon the public awareness in a subtle, yet most profound way, was that, despite the vehemence with which it had announced itself in 1960, Japanese architecture had not developed an identity of its own. Instead, under the aegis of industry and the administration, it had helped to establish Western Modernism and its innate dualism in Japan. The large central roof of the exposition became a symbol of subjection, comparable to the radial road layouts of Versailles or Karlsruhe in the Baroque age or later to the perspectives of the Champs-Elysées. It was Roland Barthes who revealed the true structure of the Japanese city in his *L'Empire des signes* in 1970. The center of the city was empty, he argued. The heart of Tokyo was the closed, inaccessible park of the Imperial Palace, a wall behind which "a holy void" was concealed.[11] Barthes succeeded in linking with this image the concept of an absent subject, a link that manifested itself precisely in those years when Postmodernism was developing. Since the Meiji period, the Japanese capital had been a showcase for Modernism imported from the West and had subsequently transformed itself into the epitome of a Postmodernism that no longer drew its inspiration from outside, but from within.

5.

The architectural fraternity again set out to "discover Japan"—rather like the millions of railway passengers who followed this slogan in the same year. The slogan itself formed part of the biggest and most successful advertising campaign ever launched by Japanese railways.

The architects began their search in their immediate surroundings. In 1971, in an essay entitled "Beyond Symbol Spaces",[12] Kazuo Shinohara wrote: "It is no longer necessary to disguise one's belief that the house is a kind of spatial creation based on a criticism of civilization." The avant-garde dissociated itself from contemporary developments and sought to create alternative models. Metabolist projects had always been distinguished by their lack of identity with a specific location, by their search for a pure, Utopian place that might be found in the sea or over existing cities—on platforms, for example. Now suddenly, the perspective narrowed. Architects concentrated their attention on their immediate surroundings. Their critique could be aimed only at the city, and more specifically, at the city of Tokyo where they lived. As a result of the centralization of the Japanese state, life was concentrated in this city—the political, economic, and cultural organs—like rays of light focused through a prismatic glass. Tokyo had transformed itself into a synonym for Japan, into a gateway to the world, where many different influences were overlaid. Here, Japan came face to face with the outside world; and conversely, it was here that the world gained its enduring impression of Japan. It was an infinitely more complex location than that evoked by the nostalgic dream landscapes of Japan National Railways' large advertising posters or the logistic schemes envisaged by the technocrats. It was a space where unmitigated capitalist exploitation had taken the rules of architecture and urban planning to the point of absurdity and, within a few years, had overthrown all standards. It was not possible to impose any kind of order on this conurbation as had been done in similar cases in Europe. On the contrary, the dynamics of the city had usurped nature, and architects could do no more than react to its unpredictable movements. Only individual responses were possible to the demands posed by the city. As a result of the process of internationalization that the Metabolists had set in motion through their astute activities, and not least through their close contacts with industry, the architectural scene had, up to that time, been able to present itself outwardly with a remarkable degree of homogeneousness. Now, suddenly, it disintegrated into a large number of different currents, directions, and preferences.

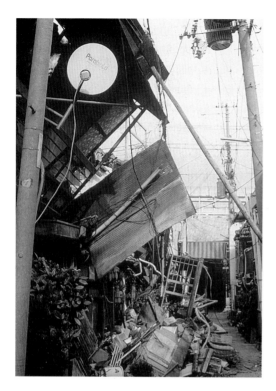

Effects of the Kobe earthquake of 1995.

bewildering death machine in the form of his Noa Building, the radical nature of which has never been achieved since. The homogeneous quality that had formerly characterized Japan disintegrated. The idealized view of a monolithic, alien block that had existed for centuries and of a largely uniform society was no longer tenable. In its place, an unexpected variety and individuality manifested itself, in addition to the technocratic and not very innovative contribution made by the administration and political classes in the form of large-scale public construction schemes. This phenomenon did not correspond in the least to the image of a consensus society, which Japan had long been seen to represent. Only 15 years later, in 1985, was Tokyo—in all its variety—to regain the homogeneous character that allowed it to be seen as a microcosm of Japan. The location had shed its skin completely and, after its successful reconsolidation, could be perceived as a prototype for the city of the 21st century. *Tokyo-ron*, the "science of the city of Tokyo", was born. New rules evolved. The Japanese capital, devoid of any center and subject, was recognized as an alternative to the European city. It was an "amoeba city" (*amebe-toshi*), as the architect Asihara Yoshinobu described it, in which the individual parts were fitted together with infinite flexibility and without any preconceptions.[14] In terms of restoration, *Tokyo-ron* discovered a place that differed fundamentally from the products of European politics; a place that set its sights on continuous, vertiginous growth instead of stagnation and the conservation of an existing state. In contrast to the generally negative views of the city that had prevailed in the 1970s and early 1980s and the skepticism toward technology that accompanied this, *Tokyo-ron* represented a positive contribution to the debate on the contemporary state of the Japanese city, as Hajime Yatsuka remarked.[15] It turned the instability of the Japanese conurbations into a positive asset. In this debate, the big Japanese cities such as Tokyo were perceived as "specifically tolerant spaces" and therewith freed from all value judgements based on conventional urban planning criteria.[16] Instead, the discussion reestablished a link with the historic city of Edo. It therefore represented a return to a *japonisme* that by this time was regarded as defunct. It was an irresponsible change of course,

The outcome was not a uniform "architecture of resistance,"[13] as the introverted "Japanese" buildings of Tadao Ando or even Toyo Ito in those years seemed to indicate. There was no return to traditional values that would have permitted a simple categorization. On the contrary, different codes existed, a set of incompatible rules that only the architects and their clients knew how to exploit. The "great story" of the city was succeeded by individual dialogues with it. These dialogues could take many different forms, ranging from completely mannerist concepts to examples of extreme reduction. The Nakagin Capsule Tower by Kisho Kurokawa (1972), for example, embodied the Metabolist architectural approach in its most pronounced form. In contrast to this, with the first sections of his Hillside Terrace, built in 1969 and 1972, Fumihiko Maki created an exclusive housing development that reveals the influence of European models in the careful design of its small open spaces and the choice of materials. At almost the same time, Seiichi Shirai, a great individualist who is little known outside Japan, created a

Street scene in Kobe, January 1995.

particularly in respect of the reception of Japanese architecture abroad, since it immediately allowed the return of Orientalism. Japan was transformed yet again into the strange and exotic country it had been at the beginning of the century in the eyes of colonialists. Now, however, it was an exoticism and sense of uniqueness to which the Japanese willingly surrendered themselves.

6.

The "Pacific century" dawned. The indomitable rise of Asia to become a new economic hyperspace focused around cosmopolitan conurbations, stimulated share markets and caused real property prices to soar. In view of its unparalleled history, Japan—and explicitly Tokyo—presented itself as a prototype. In 1987, this development came to an end. Land, a limited commodity in Japan, was much in demand and became prohibitively expensive. Companies as well as private investors successfully attempted to maximize the profits from speculative ventures on the stock exchange by depositing real property as security for large credits. This money was, in turn, reinvested on the stock exchange. It was a process

that allowed endless sums of money to be produced without any real equivalent value and which achieved a sad notoriety under the name of *zai-tech* [finance technology]. Nothing could stop the resulting hysteria. When finally not even the most banal financial restrictions existed, a cannibalization of all kinds of styles and cultures occurred. It was a game of illusion that took the breath away from visitors to Tokyo. In the words of one of the undertakings of the Parco retail trading group, the avant-garde of Japanese marketing: "Performance and novelty outweigh the concern for status and quality which occupied the previous postwar generations."[17] This development did not stop short of architecture, of course. In addition to revealing European and American influences, Tokyo blossomed anew as an "Asian" city. Japan became "exotic", but not by consciously addressing the Chinese elements of its past in a search for its roots; nor from any influences exerted by some unprecedented wave of immigration— which might have seemed inevitable for such a prosperous country. In fact, a collage-like culture of hitherto unknown sophistication developed, a three-dimensional treasure-house of quotations freely borrowed from all cultures of the world and fused together into a *mélange* in which no individual reference was identifiable any more. It was a pastiche, as Fredric Jameson described it,[18] that could exist only in an environment in which the standards no longer exist that would have allowed it to be seen as a parody.[19]

In 1991, a major exhibition in the Victoria & Albert Museum in London took stock of all these events. "Visions of Japan" presented to an astonished audience a largely unknown picture of that country. Arata Isozaki, the organizer, divided the exhibition into three parts, portraying Japan as a "realm of kitsch," a "realm of cliché" and a "realm of simulation." After years of perplexity caused by the phenomenal developments that had taken place in that country, the exhibition provided a welcome categorization. Japan again showed itself to be an extremely heterogenous but comprehensible entity: a realm, in fact! A new and official form of *japonisme* now existed. The great "void" that Roland Barthes had identified, the utter lack of content of many buildings, which had interested the Dutch architect Rem Koolhaas on many occasions, was now invested with a meaning. There was not only the precious past, which finds its modern continuation in the works of Tadao Ando; there was also a garish, neon-colored and utterly obscene common culture that filled the vacuum and commanded equal respect. The Japanese city was the apotheosis of late-capitalism, an appropriate form of expression for the *fin de siècle*. As such, it could rightly be accorded the honors of a museum and acquire general validity.

7.

In fact, however, the parameters existing at this time had again changed substantially. The exhibition, which was meant to provide a view of the state of things in Japan, had already been overtaken by reality. In 1990, with the "bursting of the bubble," the boom came to a sudden end, and subsequently, the conditions under which architecture was created in Japan changed dramatically. It was evident that there would be no continuation of the frenzied development of the 1980s. The final traumatic experience can be dated to January 17, 1995, when an earthquake devastated the city of Kobe. On March 20 of the same year, a treacherous poison attack was made on the subway system of Tokyo. The collapse of the infrastructure in Kobe destroyed the myth of technical and administrative perfection. Following on its heels, the subway attack revealed the falsity of the belief existing in Japanese society that it lived in a state of inner consensus.

In the following year, Japan presented itself at the Biennale in Venice more radically, honestly, and disconcertedly than ever. The Japanese pavilion showed exclusively scenes of destruction. Authentic sound effects, mountains of rubble and large-scale photos by Riyuji Miyamoto conveyed a lasting impression of the catastrophe that had befallen Kobe. This record of collapse was an explicit reflection of the contemporary situation. On the one hand, the exhibition demonstrated the enormous degree of disillusionment, the sense of insecurity and ensuing anxieties that the country is experiencing at present. At the same time, the pictures radiate an inexplicable intensity, a vibrancy and vitality indicative of a new beginning. The cards have been dealt anew.

Notes

1 Arata Isozaki, "Wayo Style – The Japanization Mechanism", in *Visions of Japan: 10–17*, ed. Kato Hidetoshi et al. exhibition catalogue (Tokyo, 1992; reprint of the original London catalogue).

2 Reyner Banham, *Megastructure – Urban Futures of the Recent Past*, (London, 1976), p. 45.

3 Reyner Banham and Hiroyuki Suzuki, *Modernes Bauen in Japan*, (Stuttgart, 1987), p.18.

4 Noboru Kawazoe, "The Thirty Years of Metabolists", in *Thesis, Wissenschaftliche Zeitschrift der Bauhaus-Universität Weimar*, 1998, vol. 6, pp. 147–151 (here, p. 147).

5 Alain Guiheux, *Kisho Kurokawa, Le Metabolisme 1960–1975*, (Paris, 1997), p. 30.

6 Hiroyuki Suzuki, "Japanische Architektur der Gegenwart", in Banham and Suzuki, *Modernes Bauen in Japan*, p. 7.

7 Reyner Banham, *Megastructure – Urban Futures of the Recent Past*, p. 54.

8 Jürgen Joedicke, "Realität und Utopie in der Stadtplanung", in *Bauen und Wohnen*, 1/1964, p. 68.

9 Robin Boyd, "Expo as Architecture", in *Architectural Review*, Oct. 1970, pp. 75–100 (here, p. 81).

10 Hiroyuki Suzuki, "Japanische Architektur der Gegenwart", in Banham and Suzuki, *Modernes Bauen in Japan*, p. 9.

11 Roland Barthes, *Das Reich der Zeichen*, Stuttgart, 1979, p. 50
(originally published as *L'Empire des signes*, Geneva, 1970).

12 Kazuo Shinohara, "Beyond Symbol Spaces – An Introduction
to Primary Spaces as Functional Spaces", in *Japan Architect*,
April 1971, pp. 81–88 (here, p. 81).

13 Botond Bognar, *The New Japanese Architecture*, (New York,
1990), p. 18.

14 Augustin Berque, "Die Zeitlichkeit der japanischen Stadt und die
Überwindung der Moderne", in *Überwindung der Moderne, Japan
am Ende des 20. Jahrhunderts*, ed. I. Hibiya-Kirschnerreit (Frankfurt
am Main, 1996), p. 202.

15 Hajime Yatsuka, "Japan, the Object of Dual Aestheticization",
in *Thesis, Wissenschaftliche Zeitschrift der Bauhaus-Universität
Weimar*, (1998), vol. 6, pp. 16–27 (here, p. 26).

16 Ibid.

17 Akurosu Gekkan and Shitsu Henshu (eds.), *Ima, chotaishu no jidai*
(Tokyo, 1985), pp. 43–51 (here, p. 43).

18 Fredric Jameson, "Postmodernism, or the Cultural Logic of Late
Capitalism", in *New Left Review*, no. 146 Sept./Oct. 1984,
pp. 53–92 (here, pp. 65f.).

19 Marilyn Ivy, *Discourses of the Vanishing; Modernity-Phantasm-
Japan*, (Chicago, 1995), p. 55.

The Interviews

Kisho Kurokawa

April 24, 1997

Kisho Kurokawa's extensive office was on the eleventh floor of a high-rise building. On the way to the meeting we met him coming from an exhausting design session. During the interview, Kurokawa's comprehensive response to all our questions and his expressive gestures emphasized his enthusiasm for communication and matters outside the immediate realm of architecture.

Forget the Mainstream

Christopher Knabe and Joerg Rainer Noennig: When you started your work as a Metabolist architect back in the 1960s this was considered truly avant-garde. What were the special conditions that made that possible?

Kisho Kurokawa: Being avant-garde always depends on when the architect was born. I was lucky enough that the Japanese economy really started to take off in the 1950s and 1960s. During most of this period the Prime Minister of Japan was Hayato Ikeda and he promised the nation that their salaries would double in four years. At this time the economy was increasing by twelve percent per annum. So the whole social and industrial structure changed in the 1960s and the hierarchy that classified people according to their age became chaotic. It was during these times of change that my career started. I was twenty-six when I graduated from Tokyo University and I had already created many designs—all unrealized theoretical projects.

C.K. and J.R.N.: After thirty years, is the concept of avant-garde still alive in Japan and is the preoccupation still with conceptual work?

K.K.: I think that some of the younger generation are doing quite good work based on a conceptual approach—Toyo Ito for example. Toyo Ito may be one of the successors of that generation. I think that Kenzo Tange, Fumihiko Maki, and Arata Isozaki all belong to a single generation in terms of their ideas despite the difference in their age. Their influences are predominantly Western ones. Isozaki is an extremely intelligent man. Like me Isozaki has probably published forty or fifty books but his are filled entirely with ideas from Western culture, history, and art. In his books there is nothing about Japanese culture, art, or philosophy.

C.K. and J.R.N.: Is it your aim to emphasize Japanese ideas?

K.K.: No. I started out between cultures because my childhood was just after the occupation by the

Sony Tower, Osaka, 1976.

American army. When I was at primary school we were exposed to a lot of American culture and so it was quite natural that we sometimes felt "anti-American." Ninety percent of our friends would have said "I want to go the United States, I want to study abroad." But I always stood a little outside of that and intentionally so. Later on when the economy was improving and people were talking about the possibilities of new technology, I asked myself, could this be right? How can we control technology and at the same time avoid technology controlling us? To me Metabolism is the idea of finding methods for controlling technology. My position is always counter to the mainstream.

C.K. and J.R.N.: To incorporate new technology into culture would you draw a continuous line from Metabolism to the present?

K.K.: Well, in that stream the basic concept must be life. Previously we had the machine ages with Le Corbusier, Kenzo Tange, and the whole of that old generation. Le Corbusier said the house is a machine, Eisenstein said that the film is a machine, and

Marinetti said the poem is a machine. So you see the spirit of the early twentieth century was definitely that of the "Machine Age". I started from a principle I call the "Age of Life"; then I selected "Metabolism", "Metamorphosis" and "Symbiosis" as the most important principles in life and as concepts against those of the machine. These terms define the successive periods of my work.

C.K. and J.R.N.: Your work appears as a continuous progression towards a goal, with these concepts marking the route, does this imply that they are all linked or do you differentiate between them more sharply?

K.K.: Some thirty-seven years ago I invented a new definition for the word symbiosis, *kyosei* in Japanese. My definition of symbiosis is one that encompasses opposition and contradiction and refers to new creative relationships, forms of competition, and tension. Symbiosis maintains positive relationships in which the participants necessarily understand each other despite mutual opposition. Therefore symbiosis refers to a relationship and that level of creativity which is impossible for one party to achieve alone. It is very important that participants try to broaden and share their knowledge. What was the main philosophy for the machine age? Dualism! All the sciences, technology, philosophy, art, and architecture are based on European dualism. Of course dualism is closely related to Christianity and the ideas of Kant and Descartes. Computers are also based on these ideas of dualism—zero, one, zero one—and with this limited choice are therefore not creative.

Twenty-five years ago, I declared that if a computer could deal with ambiguity then computer science could really lay claim to a new era. Now we even have "fuzzy logic" so symbiosis is becoming more and more important, not only in architecture, but also in areas such as philosophy, medicine, chemistry, and environmental studies. Symbiosis is anti-dualism and it is important to note that I was talking about this thirty years ago and was the only proponent of such an idea—now everybody's talking about it. Thirty years earlier, Japanese architects learnt everything through American and European culture particularly Le Corbusier and Walter Gropius.

Shirase Polar Expedition Museum. Left: view of the entrance courtyard; below: axonometric view.

"I am not an Architect"

C.K. and J.R.N.: If your theory can be extended to many other disciplines then surely it ceases to characterize the work of an architect as such. Do you strictly classify yourself as an architect?

K.K.: No, no, I am not an architect! Look at the new edition of my book, for example, *Each One a Hero. The Philosophy of Symbiosis.* Here I am a writer. It was first published in 1969 and since then it has been reprinted every year. I won the Grand Prix for Literature in Japan and my work has been cited as an "excellent book of philosophy" in America. This text was not about architecture at all. Sometimes I include an example of architecture in a book and that is one element of my work. But the books are not solely intended for architects to read, in fact ninety percent of the readership aren't architects. Philosophy is the main concern of these texts. I think that physical things like architecture change and die and that in seventy-five or a hundred years time my architecture will have gone. A hundred years is long enough for the life of a building. Physical things are never eternal and that's a basic premise of Japanese thinking. Nature, art, architecture, and machines have a limited longevity. The only thing that can be said to be eternal is philosophy as it invisibly enters the mind, is

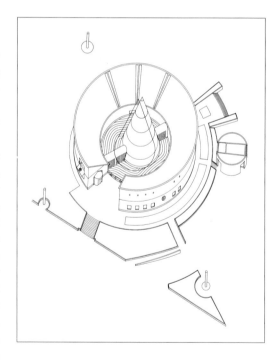

then developed and altered slightly by each personality but thereafter passes on to other minds, and stays alive. If anyone said that my architecture wasn't very striking or well developed I'd take that criticism on board. As an architectural thinker I appreciate these opinions. But at the end of the day

I consider myself first and foremost to be a philosopher and my philosophy will undoubtedly survive my buildings.

Anti-Functionalism

C.K. and J.R.N.: As well as all the books you have written the fact remains that you are also a famous architect. How do you combine your philosophy with your architectural work?

K.K.: The Athens Charter by the Congrès Internationaux d'Architecture Moderne (CIAM) produced quite a clear idea of distinction which is consistent with the ideas of the machine age, but my ideas are of a more hybrid nature.

C.K. and J.R.N.: Does symbiosis therefore refer to a special relationship between different elements and values?

K.K.: Yes. Let's take the example of mixing factories and housing which would normally be prohibited by functional town-planning theories. Ordinarily a factory should be located far away from housing, but I think that only by living with the factory can we control its pollution. If we needed a big atomic power station we should build one right in the center of Tokyo. There you can see it and feel its output and only then does it really come into people's consciousness. Under these conditions we might be able to control what's going on around us and take action concerning such things as power stations. This is the basic idea of symbiosis—the very antithesis of Functionalism.

A European World

C.K. and J.R.N.: Rather than looking for synthesis and eliminating cultural differences, do you strive to promote difference in order to retain contradiction and confrontation as a creative driving force?

K.K.: Let's put it this way, my idea of architecture is more flexible. At the beginning of Metabolism I looked at the Katsura Detached Palace as a text: this is a Japanese masterpiece. The palace has been extended twice in one hundred and fifty years, by contrast with a European masterpiece that generally

has to stand forever untouched. This is just one fundamental difference between European and Asian or Japanese philosophy and how it is applied to buildings. For a long time now Asian countries have interpreted progress according to the European standard, and that's why developing countries try to copy European architecture. Japan, China, India, and other developing nations have been trying to close up what they see as a gap between themselves and Europe and lessening this distance equates with success. But what happens after a hundred years of pursuing this line? The whole world will be European! For me this would mark the loss of diversity and my basic premise is a symbiosis of cultures, retaining each in its own right and with equal importance, be it European, Islamic, Japanese, or any other.

A culture's importance should not be decided by the country's economic power. Once Egypt was very influential and gradually became less so in terms of its economy, but its culture still remains precious and should be regarded differently from the country's economic development. I also believe that basic human happiness depends on retaining cultural diversity. Tange, Isozaki, and Maki all succeeded in catching up with European and American culture. I needed a different starting point and although I had studied and admired European culture I was deeply interested in Japanese culture and philosophy. I also devoted time to learning Sanskrit so that I could read Indian philosophy. The reason behind creating a philosophy that greatly differs from that of the early twentieth century is simply my way of bringing disparate things together. My career now spans some thirty-seven years; it has been clearly directed like fate. I wasn't making architecture for myself like Tadao Ando who is always pursuing his own style. My style is always different, always new and varying in shape because of this gathering of different elements, cultures, functions, and locations.

Twenty-First Century Architect

C.K. and J.R.N.: Once you described yourself as a social engineer and not as an architect. Can you explain this?

Nova Municipal
Museum

K.K.: I'm a philosopher first!

C.K. and J.R.N.: Why do you continue to make architecture at all?

K.K.: Because a philosopher can work in other professions at the same time. Firstly a philosopher and then a physicist, violinist, or fashion designer—that's what can be done. People who teach philosophy are not philosophers in their own right. Explaining Kant or Descartes is teaching but I am a real philosopher because I'm engaged in creating a philosophy by myself. Of course I am at the same time an architect, but one distinguished from others by my role as philosopher.

C.K. and J.R.N.: Is the philosopher the model architect for the next century?

K.K.: Yes. The most important thing for the twenty-first century architect is that he should be a philosopher. This architect must think about what type of spirit we should have in the next century, what people's desires are and what era we are living in. We should understand that we can be very happy and if not there will be a great deal of social anxiety. The "architect-philosopher"—you can certainly place me under that heading.

C.K. and J.R.N.: This challenges the image of the profession completely. Do you reject the image of the architect who makes "artistic" architecture?

K.K.: Yes. If someone is only an architect he is like an artist whose paintings are basically very beautiful with good perspective and so on. His hands might be very magical but not philosophical. I don't respect this definition of an architect's life.

C.K. and J.R.N.: What would you describe as your most important architectural heritage—your books or the architecture itself?

K.K.: I would say that the philosophy is most important, so in that case the books outweigh the architecture. If this book is in a library, the library itself may change—they can tear down the building and let another architect build a new library—but the book will remain the same.

C.K. and J.R.N.: Don't you place any trust in architects?

K.K.: Only in the new type.

C.K. and J.R.N.: How else would you characterize the "new architect"?

K.K.: The new architect will have to consider how society wants to live in modern times. One consideration is that people now seek to live in a city comfortably, in a city that is stimulating. I for one would definitely like to live in a city that could deliver a lot of stimulus, then I could be a more creative man. At present the professional architects who are preoccupied with structural engineering,

Wakayama Prefectural Museum, 1996

beautiful facades and functions, make a sort of mechanical suit of architecture. Because of the professional architect we don't currently have the kind of city that I have described. The professional architect is too bound to his own profession, never studying other professions or trying to understand them. In general architects are people without ears or mouths who cannot take on information from other professions any more than they can listen to the ideas of the layman, the real people! By contrast I often think about sociology, economics, or history. The twenty-first century architect will be more dynamic, still capable of living up to his profession but working the architecture towards real people's requirements. I think this will lead to a more dramatic and stimulating type of architecture—houses should be more lively. Let's face it you only have this life once.

C.K. and J.R.N.: Does that mean that architecture should be more like art?

K.K.: No I don't think so. It is to do with the type of communication between ordinary people and architects. It is very different from art. If the client wants art they go to a famous architect to get a kind of unique home architecture. This client never proposes a program, cost effects, or his own desires but asks the architect to design in their own style, saying "please give me a masterpiece!" What happens then is that the architect has *carte blanche* to create architecture for himself, as Ando does. The architecture will only be an expression of the architect's identity. This is the same in Paris, Switzerland, Tokyo, or anywhere else at present, using the same pure language and the same material.

Roots

C.K. and J.R.N.: What are the basic roots of your philosophy?

K.K.: Buddhism. I studied symbiosis [*kyosei*] from junior high school and the teacher was a very famous Buddhist philosopher, Shiyo Keitekyo, who graduated from Tokyo University and had studied Indian Buddhism. At this time a new Buddhist movement had started and was in fact called "Symbiosis": this is my deepest root. My own philosophy of symbiosis is not primarily related to Buddhism although it is an important influence. Now the idea has come into the realm of medical studies, quantum theory, and biology and scholars from all disciplines are now discussing symbiosis.

C.K. and J.R.N.: Would you regard symbiosis as a distinct type of radicalism?

K.K.: Yes, but sometimes people misunderstand my philosophy of symbiosis and have difficulty making sense of it, thinking of it as eclectic idealism, or else they say that it is against Christianity and is a type of vandalism—how ridiculous to think of Buddhism as vandalism! We cannot accept such an idea in Buddhism. In Japan it is not totally uncommon for people to be Buddhist, Christian, and Muslim all at the same time if they wish. This might sound strange but it's quite possible. One Buddhist actually became a teacher of Islamic philosophy at Cairo University. This mixing is perfectly acceptable to Buddhist society. Buddhism is very open-minded and not at all exclusive. Buddha lives in every part of the universe, in you, me, inside a pen, a book, inside clouds; and instead of one god in the position of creator, we would say that each of us and every part of nature is also a creator: it is a symbolic relationship. Some ten thousand texts were written on Buddhism between pre-Christian times and the fourth century, with each philosopher following on from their predecessor. These were "Consciousness only" doctrines and this is my background.

Spiritual Architecture

C.K. and J.R.N.: What do you see as an appropriate order for society in the next century?

K.K.: I think that Japan is actually at the center of this movement towards a new order. Now we can understand why the Japanese economy has recently been one of the best in the world, and that is clearly because of Japan's wealth. What does money mean? Money creates money. Then the bubble economy crashed and there was nothing left. Following this most people now understand that human beings need to rely on things other than money and material wealth. So spirit and inspiration now seem more important for living through difficult periods in life. What will inspire people? What will inspire the architects themselves? I don't think that making a big project, creating a house for rich people or driving a fancy car will continue to be stimulating or fulfilling. Even working on a small scale we have to create a more spiritual architecture. Interest in a spiritually oriented life is now really starting to take

off. It is a departure from the materialistic lifestyle towards a more spiritual one.

C.K. and J.R.N.: What is characteristic of this new sort of lifestyle?

K.K.: In present times the changes in what people want are quite interesting because they are coherent with the Japanese culture of the past and are based on the same idea of spiritual lifestyle that is part of our history. Japanese people are once again found thinking in more traditional ways more concerned with the intangible, the spiritual, the sensitive, and the aesthetic than with the material. This shift in attitude explains how we can bridge the gap between history and the present, now that we are less fixed to material things. Look at the Ise Shrine [in Mie prefecture] that was originally built in the seventh century but is continually rebuilt every twenty years and we still claim it is the same shrine. It is one thousand two hundred years of history and at the same time it is always new! [In Japan, the preservation of form and process supersedes the preservation of the material structure itself and therefore the rebuilt Ise Shrine can always be seen to be the original.] Another example is the Daibutsu-den Hall of Todai-ji Temple, this is a national treasure built in the eighth century and is considered to be our oldest wooden structure despite being rebuilt having burnt down two hundred years ago.

C.K. and J.R.N.: If it is physically new, can it still truly be regarded as the oldest?

K.K.: Yes of course, and this time they didn't even replicate the original design but built it totally differently—even the size is only seventy percent of the original. Imagine if that happened in Europe—I think people would refuse to accept it as the original architecture.

C.K. and J.R.N.: This would be thought of as a fake, as imitation, or as deceptive in Europe.

K.K.: "Not original!"—that's something the Japanese would never say. We can change the design and the size a thousand years into its existence, and though strictly speaking it might not be true to call it the original, neither is it a lie. It's simply a different way of thinking and as I have already mentioned, I try to be a philosopher not an architect, because architectural shape is nothing and the architect is nothing. Buildings can last up to several hundred

Kuala Lumpur International Airport, Malaysia, 1999, under construction.

years at most but philosophy? Philosophy lasts for thousands of years and unlike buildings can travel the world over.

Philosophical Heritage

C.K. and J.R.N.: You intensively rework and redefine your own career. Do you feel this is central for your work's continuity and progress?

K.K.: Yes. Take these woodblock prints of mine as an example. *Architecture in the World of Images* represents twenty of my most significant prints. Each has taken me one year to complete so that's essentially twenty years work. The paper I used is a traditional *ukiyo-e* paper [*ukiyo-e* literally means "pictures of the floating world", and is a style of painting and printing made popular in the eighteenth and nineteenth centuries]. That type of paper is the same that *ukiyo-e* masters such as Katsushika Hokusai and Ando Hiroshige used. An exhibition of my woodblock prints traveled all over the world, not as the work of an architect, but as that of an artist.

C.K. and J.R.N.: Do some of the titles of your prints connect your feelings about philosophy to buildings you have made, in particular "Cell" and "Periphery"?

K.K.: I would place the titles somewhere in between—it is not that easy to say. My current search revolves around thinking of how I can pass on my work in all its different aspects to the next generation. The problem is that I am still avant-garde and not everyone understands me, but one of my goals is definitely to pass on my heritage. After my death it is your role to study what I did.

C.K. and J.R.N.: Has your own view on the avant-garde changed?

K.K.: I think so. When Europeans reach the age of sixty they are no longer avant-garde. But I am still fighting. [Kurokawa is in his sixties.] I have had many of my projects remain unrealized but I keep working. It is a similar situation now to that at the beginning of my career, and I am still not seriously established. Any established architect would now only make projects through invitation to competitions, but you can see that I am still doing open competitions, I am still training myself and that's the spirit of avant-garde. If you are only concerned about realizing the full project then your sense of avant-garde will disappear.

Riken Yamamoto

June 18, 1997

Staff numbers and space in Riken Yamamoto's offices have much increased recently as a result of competition success and a resulting increase in commissions. In this busy environment Yamamoto was at first somewhat skeptical about the interview. However during the discussions he became more and more involved in the matters at hand, revealing some far-reaching concerns about the fundamentals of today's architecture.

Christopher Knabe and Joerg Rainer Noennig: The port of Yokohama retains many traces of foreign culture and was recently host to an international competition to design the port terminal in which you won second prize. Do you feel Yokohama differs greatly from other Japanese cities because of these foreign influences?

Riken Yamamoto: Nowadays, Yokohama isn't that different from other cities in Japan. Tokyo now combines many places such as Saitama, Chiba, and Yokohama and we call this the "doughnut" phenomenon—these cities encircle Tokyo and form its sub-cities. They are actually what we term dormitory towns, places where people who work in the city go home just to sleep. The financial strength is now concentrated in Tokyo's geographic center, which I think is an awful situation. Before World War II these sub-cities had their own identities, but today it is hard to tell them apart. Cities like Saitama and Chiba are now described only in terms of their geographic relationship to Tokyo and the time it takes to reach

them from the center. Land prices run in bands that circle Tokyo, and are calculated similarly by their distance from the center.

C.K. and J.R.N.: Yokohama has a spectacular new port side. Isn't it now important enough to be considered a city or center in its own right?

R.Y.: We call cities such as Makuhari or Yokohama's port town, "sub-centers". I think that the government had it in mind to recreate Yokohama as a new city center, but Tokyo still retains this sole position.

C.K. and J.R.N.: Unlike the sub-centers of Shinjuku or Shibuya, the newly built Makuhari seems very empty and silent by comparison.

R.Y.: "MM21" [Minato Mirai 21st Century], the new port town of Yokohama, is similar to Makuhari in this sense. The reason for this in Yokohama is that the government decided not to include housing in the area so it's predominantly commercial.

C.K. and J.R.N.: How did you feel about Yokohama's change of image?

Yokohama Exotic Showcase, 1989. Night view of temporary scaffolding structure.

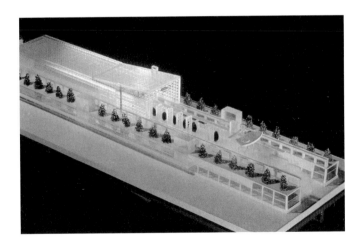

Yokohama International Sea Terminal, 1995.
Competition entry model.

R.Y.: I have lived there since I was four years old [Yamamoto is now in his forties]. Since 1950, the situation for most Japanese cities has been changed drastically by government intervention, and this didn't only affect Yokohama. Most cities had certain traditional structures, and the government changed these to provide better conditions for infrastructure, highways, railroad tracks, and traffic in general. With the emphasis placed on traffic systems, the government neglected to provide communal spaces and public facilities for people. I lived in a small district in Yokohama. In front of my home there used to be a very narrow street, about four meters wide, this was suddenly extended to twenty-four meters

Ryokuen-toshi Inter-junction city, Yokohama, 1992–94. Above left: aerial view; top right: public through-pass; above right: view from the station.

and became almost like a highway! This caused the destruction of the small social community that used to be there. Regardless of this dramatic change we were still supposed to live next to this road, and this type of thing happened in all the cities. In the 1960s, Yokohama provided me with a training ground for working in urban situations.

C.K. and J.R.N.: In Japan there are no squares or centers as there are in European cities where people can gather. When these places disappear it disrupts social functions.

R.Y.: That's right. Tokyo and Yokohama are now very different from European models. I taught in Berlin, and there I found many residential areas around the center, demonstrating that it is still possible to live in the middle of a city. I think that new city planning should incorporate both residential and commercial considerations at the same time. Presently this isn't happening and in Yokohama's port city there simply isn't any room for a housing area now, so in this case it's too late. One strong idea

that has been adopted from nineteenth-century Europe is that of the "garden city", which draws a distinction between working and dwelling areas, Japan really seems to have taken that on board.

C.K. and J.R.N.: In Berlin the building law states that twenty percent of building volume should be given over to residential use.

R.Y.: That's certainly a good idea.

Inter-Junction City

C.K. and J.R.N.: In your Ryokuen-toshi "inter-junction" project you tried to connect various functions, combining shopping areas, business facilities, and housing. Was it a success?

R.Y.: Not yet! It takes time to assess if a project is working, but I really hope that it will.

C.K. and J.R.N.: A project of that scale can't be realized all at once. I imagine the shops, for instance, would appear at a later stage than the housing.

Could you foresee how long it would take to develop in its entirety?

R.Y.: It will take another three or four years. There are eight buildings around the station that are complete, a few shops are rented but there is still vacant business space, so some have said it won't be a successful project. But recently things have changed, with some restaurants and shops developing really well inside this project. Getting this far has taken four years, so I am confident that in another four years the site will see much more positive development.

C.K. and J.R.N.: This project is discussed in your essay "Cell City". "Inter-junction city" is still very young—only six years old. What's the next step in its development?

R.Y.: The developer of this city is in fact a private company, the Sagami Railroad Company, and to date the local government hasn't got involved. I think that if the government could be encouraged to participate in the venture, things could change dramatically, and they could provide communal features like a small library for example. Hopefully the government will respond within the next five or six years.

C.K. and J.R.N.: You once said you thought that it was pointless to try and create "unique" architecture. How did you conceive this project?

R.Y.: Japanese commercial buildings are usually thought of as monuments. Private buildings in particular are designed to be as unique as possible and are, in a sense, a monument to the owners themselves. You could call this "self-satisfied monumentalism". The idea behind this kind of monumentalism is that it functions as a signature. For that very reason you can find a lot of peculiar or extravagant buildings, which are monuments in a Japanese city, and no consideration is given to the surrounding area.

C.K. and J.R.N.: In contrast to this idea, you have begun with a framework and structures can be "plugged" into this.

R.Y.: I created a rule governing the entire scheme. If I make a structure successfully, then this structure automatically creates the city from there on, provided that the landowners follow the rules that I've prescribed. In the Ryokuen-toshi scheme one common condition existed, and this was that each building possessed a public through-pass which acted as passageway linking each building.

C.K. and J.R.N.: You had proposed this rule as the urban planning and then the landowners chose you to design all the buildings.

R.Y.: Before this project was decided upon I told the landowners that they could choose any architect they wanted, with the only proviso being that they should follow this through-pass rule. Fortunately, after accepting the project, they chose me to see it through!

Intense Space

C.K. and J.R.N.: You seem to be interested in "intense" space. From where do you derive your spatial images?

R.Y.: Japanese cities usually develop along the roadside. Sites are partitioned into numerous lots. Typically, the buildings are set onto the lots, covering approximately eighty percent of the ground; the remaining land is needed for the buildings' construction. This means that very narrow strips of only one or two meters separate the buildings. This is a feature of Tokyo and different from Europe where you quite often have a continuous building or at least a continuous facade, [or strict rules regarding urban planning]. If you have buildings separated like this, each owner can make their own "monumental" or at least unique, house.

C.K. and J.R.N.: You seem to accept this condition.

R.Y.: Yes, but I have thought about how to use these spaces in between. I might be able to connect separate buildings with these spaces in between, and the spaces might develop into new streets.

Illusions of Architecture

C.K. and J.R.N.: In your "Cell City" essay you wrote: "We work under the illusion that architecture is something to be seen, in fact nobody looks at architecture." Is that how you like to work—assuming the architecture goes unnoticed, not planning "artistic" architecture as much as providing a set of conditions

"Rotunda" building, Yokohama, 1987.

European cities were designed with symbolic reference to the ruler, dictator, or monarch. With this type of layout, you can detect a hierarchy of clearly distinct zones. At the top, or center, sits the monarch and this is the most powerful city structure.

Making New Communities

C.K. and J.R.N.: A feature of your work is how concrete structures change into light construction towards the top of the buildings, and almost dissolve into the air. These buildings are less individual than the "monuments"—they almost disappear.

R.Y.: I have employed designs like this for ten years, since the "Gazebo" and "Rotunda" buildings, and my "Hamlet" residential complex which involves a similar concept. Having the commercial facilities in the lower area and the living area above is an idea I first had over thirty years ago, when I still lived on a narrow street. At that time there were many people

"Hamlet" Residential Complex, Tokyo, 1988.
Above: aerial view; below: roof membrane structure.

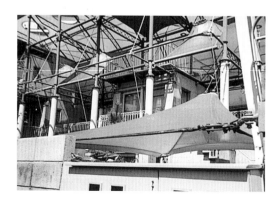

for the architecture to follow, and then letting the city develop by itself?

R.Y.: That's one of my basic principles.

C.K. and J.R.N.: During your studies you took part in field trips with Hiroshi Hara's laboratory, that took you through Europe and a number of Third World countries. How did this affect your architecture?

R.Y.: This was a great experience, especially the Islamic cities we traveled through. These cities were in some ways close to traditional Japanese city spaces, especially the bazaars, where you pass through a lot of small streets with shops and homes.

C.K. and J.R.N.: You have said that the modern idea of the city, formulated by CIAM in the Athens Charter [1933], is completely invalid and cannot address the conditions of present day Asia.

R.Y.: Before the modern era European cities had patterns of long straight streets flanked by monumental buildings. The axes were mainly directed towards the city center, as for example Baron Haussmann created in Paris. Even before the nineteenth century, living on the upper floors of these houses, and this made the top floors into a very special area. Sometimes neighbors met there to pass the time of day. There's an immense contrast between the zones of such houses. At the base you have the parts of the building that belong to the city space and the street, but on the upper floors the space belongs to the community that live there. Now I'm attempting to make a city with this type of living space.

C.K. and J.R.N.: Does the sense of community and neighborliness you mention still exist at all in Japan?

R.Y.: Community in present day Japan is remarkably difficult to explain. Many feel that there isn't actually any community, that it has disintegrated. It is true that there is nothing like the sense of community of the nineteenth century left in Japan. I can conceive community in two basic ways: either we should try to create a community once again, or we decide that community isn't necessary. The latter would imply that everyone could live by themselves, the case of the absolute individual. We might achieve a situation in which we can enjoy individuality similar to the way in which people did in the late nineteenth and early twentieth centuries.

C.K. and J.R.N.: In Japan the term "community" is not confined to family, as it is also incorporated in the work environment under the expression *uchi no kaisha* [literally: *house/home company*, which means workplace], so that both family and workplace share the function of community. Does this varied application of community make its definition problematic?

R.Y.: Yes it is extremely difficult to fix an interpretation of community.

I certainly think we should create new communities that differ from those of the nineteenth century. I think that it's unnecessary to recreate communities as such, but rather to design in a way that members of a family or community can live independently, with the option of coming together in another space in the design as they choose. As far as I'm concerned this approach to community is preferable. Toyo Ito, on the other hand, teaches that people should enjoy individual life in a more literal sense because he thinks that it is more fulfilling.

C.K. and J.R.N.: Ito called that idea "the city nomad," for people who can live anywhere without belonging to a community at all.

R.Y.: That's right and I approve of the idea if it is engaged as a model for young people who are strong and healthy and living in Tokyo. This idea couldn't be applied broadly as it can't accommodate the needs of young children, the elderly, or the handicapped, who each require some degree of care and therefore community.

C.K. and J.R.N.: Is your emphasis then, on a "community of individuals"?

R.Y.: Yes it is. I think that we should make new communities that are distinctly different from those of the last two centuries. It must be possible to live by yourself and with someone at the same time. Right in the middle of the city there are children and handicapped people and there is presently no real way of addressing their special needs. There isn't a housing model that can cope with this type of consideration and Toyo Ito's "nomad" model simply denies participation in such a community.

A New Housing Model—A New Society

C.K. and J.R.N.: Do you think that architects can accommodate social change and even play a part in it?

R.Y.: Yes and in some respects that is very easy. Proposing new housing models for the family or the individual is all that has been called for to date. Take the Japanese *"living, dining, kitchen"* (LDK) designs, which accommodate the members of one family with the most basic requirements, or the single room mansion, an apartment, which is the single person's equivalent. In Tokyo at the moment there are only two models available, so an alternative idea has to be developed. I favor a third concept. With my Hotakubo estate, which isn't complete yet, I suggested to the government that we incorporate community functions like a nursery, kindergarten, a library, and convenience stores. Building things without the city's needs in mind won't alleviate the problems of a city.

C.K. and J.R.N.: Hotakubo is part of the development of the whole area called the Kumamoto Artpolis and the architects involved in this appear to be initiating change. This might be termed avantgarde: would you include yourself as avantgarde?

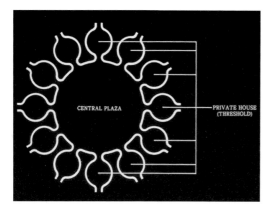

Hotakubo Public Housing, Kumamoto, 1991.
Above: conceptual drawing; below: aerial view; bottom: central plaza.

R.Y.: I can accept that, but it's not simply a case of being or not being avant-garde: architects have to consider their responsibilities and not merely design. Architects must be open to suggestions when working on new houses. At present it is important to work out how to overcome these two models of the family and the individual. A new approach must not only combine the family and the individual but must also be distinct from both nineteenth century and Russian Constructivist models.

C.K. and J.R.N.: How do you think a new model might affect people?

R.Y.: Most people haven't been exposed to a new model for society and still believe that they have to live as a family—the nuclear family. The type of housing they occupy is usually expensive because of the incredibly high land prices, whereas community houses are actually more economical. It is very difficult to change society with architecture, but we can at least suggest an alternative social image. I feel that there is a huge demand to change this society but there is no obvious way of achieving this, and added to this Japanese society is very rigid. Architects can only propose a shape, the place, the design or a new model to communicate this but it's difficult to foresee if this would be adopted or if it would instigate social change. As far as I'm concerned I'm quite convinced that ordinary people would choose an alternative way of living, were it made available to them.

C.K. and J.R.N.: You refer to your own projects as highly experimental buildings.

R.Y.: Yes that's exactly right, every building should be an experiment and this is a primary condition for evolution. Sometimes one small house is enough to set change in motion!

C.K. and J.R.N.: Itsuko Hasegawa built a new cultural center for the people of Sumida-ku in Tokyo. In her development of this project, Hasegawa became very involved with the local people through discussing their needs. This communication between the architect and those who will be using the buildings seems to be a new area of concern for architecture in Japan.

R.Y.: Itsuko Hasegawa is often brilliant as an architectural "fashion designer." She continuously tries to change the program as with the Shonandai and Sumida culture centers. Another architect, Toyo Ito, is without doubt challenging new architecture in a different way. His attempts towards new programs are somehow stronger; his way of design is closely related to the program that he's developed and this is something I occasionally miss in the works of Hasegawa.

Closing the Gap

C.K. and J.R.N.: You don't seem very interested in "form" as such. Can you explain this?

R.Y.: Form can be separated from the program and the model, and form can be regarded as belonging to fashion, which is not my primary concern. If a form isn't thought of as fashionable today, it might well be considered the height of architectural fashion in ten or more years time.

C.K. and J.R.N.: In your work the distance between concept and design is almost non-existent. Do you hope to continue to close the gap in your strategies for urban design?

R.Y.: Yes and I hope that this becomes more obvious. I incorporate the same concept for urban planning and the design details. It is quite possible to do so despite being complicated. I would actually like to design moving directly from the program to the details.

Eternal Optimist

C.K. and J.R.N.: You were a guest critic at Yokohama's National University last year [1996]. What do you feel about the education of architects in Japan?

R.Y.: Japanese universities have many problems: the education in architecture is by and large engineering—and not design—orientated. Most students graduating from an architectural course will be employed by construction companies for engineering work or as civil servants—very few of them become real architects. This means that university professors constantly discuss how to educate students and direct them into careers as architects. As a teacher, I feel this dilemma myself. Alongside promoting the idea that architects can change society, I also try to teach them a kind of social responsibility. The trouble is that most students actually want to become engineers, and more than this, they believe that society is rigid and unchangeable.

C.K. and J.R.N.: You call your own architecture "optimistic."

R.Y.: Yes, and I am convinced that my architecture is truly optimistic.

Kengo Kuma

June 23, 1997

Against a backdrop of densely packed bookshelves—
symbolic perhaps of his interest in the architecture of
both past and present—Kengo Kuma revealed during
this interview his very individual stance as a newcomer
on the Japanese scene.

Theoretical Impact

Christopher Knabe and Joerg Rainer Noennig: You studied at Columbia University, which is famous for its theoretical approach to architecture. Can you apply that approach to your work in Japan?

Kengo Kuma: In Japan my teacher was Hiroshi Hara and his approach is also very theoretical, so it was nothing exceptional. Basically both the approaches of Hiroshi Hara and that of Columbia University have the same type of theoretical considerations.

C.K. and J.R.N.: Does having studied both in Japan and abroad give your architecture an international outlook?

K.K.: Yes, to a degree, and that is something I learned from Bernard Tschumi, Kenneth Frampton, and Douglas Dartun. At Columbia I was often involved in discussions with Douglas Dartun and this was a great and fruitful experience for me. Douglas and I are of the same generation [in their forties] and he was a good friend of mine. Sadly he passed

away two years ago. Some three or four years ago *a+u* magazine published a special issue about his work and he was without doubt an absolutely theoretical architect. His drawings and theory were always excellent. He also wrote a book called *Condemned Architecture* published by Princeton University Press.

C.K. and J.R.N.: Columbia University has a reputation for being very up to date with its publications, videos, and panel talks, which focus largely on "media architecture". How did you engage with what you learnt on your return to Japan?

K.K.: When I came back from Columbia I published a book called *10 Houses*, presently only available in Japanese. This was my first book and it became very popular, its circulation now runs to some twenty thousand issues. The book describes ten types of Japanese house. The intention was to include house designs that are not representative of each architect's style and in doing so to say

Water/Glass Villa, 1997. View of lounge surrounded by a sheet of water which stretches into the Pacific Ocean.

something different about each architect's work. An architect's style has come to mean something like their "brand" or "fashion" as in the architecture of Tadao Ando.

C.K. and J.R.N.: So this work was your first attempt towards making "non-style" architecture?

K.K.: Yes, you could say so. Before my generation, designing small houses was the only way of becoming an architect. Today university students believe they could even change the world by designing a small house, and Tadao Ando is representative of such thinking. For my part, I really don't think that designing a house can be revolutionary any longer, and certainly not for the new generation of architects.

C.K. and J.R.N.: If a small house is no longer the starting point for new architects, how else might they begin?

K.K.: One idea is to try and have a book published; another is to think about urban questions and then make designs, an exhibition, or a video presentation

around them. This type of approach will prove to be much more influential and far reaching than starting from a house, and of course that is my own approach.

Media Architect

C.K. and J.R.N.: Architecture is traditionally thought of as a physical entity, something monumental or permanent. However you seem concerned with a perception of it as "media architecture", something that is not an end in itself.

K.K.: That's right, and coming back from Columbia "media architecture" was my strongest belief and a concept I clearly wanted to follow. One of my classmates was Kyoshi Takeyama, now professor at Kyoto University and he greatly admired Tadao Ando – even going as far as calling him a god. I talked with Kyoshi Takeyama a great deal. We discussed the validity of the "small houses" approach to architecture which I

Kobori Enshu. Garden in the Datokuji Temple, Kyoto.

am completely against. "Media architecture" is more significant and frees the architect from their architect style. In future architects will inevitably have to develop themselves as some type of media designer rather than as material designers.

C.K. and J.R.N.: There are various ways to present architecture using perspective, axonometric images, plans, and CAD animation, and these have usually been distinct from architecture itself. Now you intermingle them, and presentation and architecture coincide.

K.K.: What I want to highlight is the advantage for architects in using real and virtual media at the same time. Any computer designer is restricted to virtual media, but if you combine both real and virtual entities you can reach a higher level of presentation and influence in architecture. Information held in the real material is condensed by the virtual information. Tangible things contain various amounts of information and architecture can exploit that efficiently by means of the new media.

C.K. and J.R.N.: A theme in current architecture is how it is translated into digital media and how this digital expression can be translated back into material architecture. In your Eco-park project you coined the term "particle-ization" which directly refers to the digital world.

K.K.: That translation, in both directions, actually gives rise to a new kind of architecture. In ordinary terms digital architecture means CAD, but that keeps these two worlds [digital and material] separate. If these two aspects are combined they will find that they have in fact strengthened one another.

C.K. and J.R.N.: In your essay, "Seen and to be Seen" you emphasize reversing some ways of seeing, engaging real and virtual ways of seeing and overlapping them. Doesn't this mean the borderline between the ways becomes unclear?

K.K.: As far as I'm concerned the borderline is intentionally uncertain. Information depends essentially on various data and on the electron as a type of material. We cannot see this but nevertheless regard

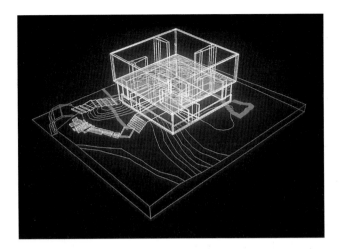

Space Design of Japan Pavilion at the Venice Biennale, 1995. Left: aerial view computer drawing; below: interior wooden path over a sheet of water.

it as something material, and yes, the borderline is very ambiguous.

Design for Consciousness

C.K. and J.R.N.: To what degree is your approach to architecture influenced by your own culture?

K.K.: I have drawn a great deal from traditional Japanese architecture. In Japan architecture is essentially the science of consciousness and the science of the body. You can say that gardening, lifestyle, and architecture are not to be separated but are rather to be conceived as an entire world. Kobori

Enshu [1579–1647] was an architect and gardener in the Edo period [1615–1867]. He was one of the designers of the Katsura Detached Palace in Kyoto, as well as being an accomplished tea ceremony master. For him architecture, the garden, and the tea ceremony were all one and the same. He saw everything as part of a design for consciousness in the human mind. His design process began from considerations about the art of the tea ceremony and this meant calculating how people perceive and experience space, time, and nature. [The art of the Japanese tea ceremony lies in a combination of nature and traditional arts. It includes not only the serving and drinking of tea but also calligraphy, poetry, and ceramics, and great reverence is given to both the space in which it is held and a sense of spiritual discipline.] It may seem surprising but to Kobori Enshu there was no discrepancy between designing gardens and designing space for tea ceremonies.

C.K. and J.R.N.: It can be concluded then that in Japan considerations about space are not limited to material things but include both people's actions in these spaces and their perception of a given environment.

K.K.: Yes, and I would even go as far as describing Kobori Enshu as a "software designer". The important thing is that hardware is a part of software.

C.K. and J.R.N.: Your work is dazzling in the way in which it combines traditional Japanese elements with contemporary ones, and this can also be seen in your work outside Japan.

K.K.: That's right, in Venice for example there is the Biennale Pavilion for which I drew on the concept of *suki* [pertaining to considerations of space] for the tea ceremony, where the sense of space takes precedence over the architecture itself. All I made was a small passageway over the water. What I wanted to do was to design more for the consciousness of people than for the actual space. I was thinking of consciousness in the sense that in every corner a new world opens. That fusion of different worlds is fundamental to the Katsura Detached Palace or to any Japanese garden; it is a layering of many worlds. When video artist Nam June Paik visited the Biennale Pavilion he commented that the experience of it was similar to that which he felt about the Katsura Detached Palace. He is sensitive and perceptive about such matters. At first I asked people to walk barefoot along the passageway at the Biennale because the feeling of the material underfoot is really important and it must be experienced directly by the skin—it is a real multimedia experience!

No Shoes Please!

C.K. and J.R.N.: Your architecture has a great tactile quality, so much so that it could be argued that the architecture itself is subordinate to people's feelings and experience of it.

K.K.: Yes, my work has emphasized its tactile features, but I'm not sure that everyone understands this. On the opening day of the Biennale Pavilion, people complained about having to take their shoes off! So you see there was some confusion. The committee of the Venice Biennale asked me to allow people to leave their shoes on, and this struck me as a major difference between Western and Japanese culture. In Japan taking off your shoes is no problem. Walking barefoot gives you a deeper sensation, which is an experience of architecture outside of or beyond the immediate architecture.

C.K. and J.R.N.: Do you think that your work can only be fully understood and applied in Japan?

K.K.: No, I don't think so. It's just a matter of introducing different concepts and materials. When I lived in New York and studied at Columbia I had to bring some *tatami* mats as they are difficult to come by abroad. In New York there are plenty of Japanese restaurants with *shoji* [paper-covered sliding doors] but no *tatami* mats. Western people seem to understand Japanese culture only as a style but *tatami* change the perception of space, and this challenges some of the basics for Western people. I finally got two *tatami* mats from a Californian carpenter who was originally from Japan. Each time friends visited my apartment we sat at first on the *tatami*, and I soon realized that this is the best space to have discussions about differences in cultures.

C.K. and J.R.N.: Japanese architecture is considered to be amongst the most sophisticated and the *tatami* mats are a good historical as well as present example of this. How do you manage to combine such sophistication with originality in your own work?

K.K.: Sophistication is a basic characteristic in Japanese culture. Japanese sophistication has been part of what keeps it a closed culture. With the tea ceremony, for example, another world emerges and people outside Japan can hardly understand its meaning. I feel that sophistication works in the wrong way in our culture and so I aim to select key concepts in Japanese culture and translate them into a more open, international vocabulary.

C.K. and J.R.N.: Do you incorporate any other traditional elements into your own living space, while combining some new approach, a tearoom perhaps?

Yusuhara's Visitor's Center, 1994.

K.K.: Yes, I have—my *chashitsu* [tearoom], it is made using special *shoji* with translucent plastics. The disappearance of detail is essential to my work; this is also a fundamental feature of traditional Japanese architecture. I think that the disappearance of detail is a very international concept too.

C.K. and J.R.N.: Rem Koolhaas wrote that the architecture of detail is "old architecture".

K.K.: While we are talking about disappearance let me explain my latest design. The project involves a site with a small mountain by a river—you won't find any architecture there just a mountain with a small slit I created through which people can view the river.

C.K. and J.R.N.: Making architecture "disappear" and working a lot with nature might point to difficulties for you when working in a metropolis such as Tokyo. Is that the case?

K.K.: The current situation for architects is a tough one, right across the board, and for me designing in Tokyo is definitely difficult. I have many projects in the countryside but not in Tokyo. Since I take the position of celebrating "weak" architecture and have an affinity with nature, you can see that the demands of Tokyo and its "strong" architecture are problematic for me. My work is based on a combination of civil engineering, landscape design, and architecture. The landscape work of Kevin Roche and in particular his Oakland Museum has had a great impact on me. His work is a combination of landscape and museum. That kind of mixed-media work has deeply influenced my own architecture. In twentieth-century Western history, landscape and architecture became opposites but in Japanese history the landscape and the "object" or architecture have never functioned as opposites, they have always worked as one whole entity. I think that this separation of elements is peculiar to Western ideas.

Pure Architecture

C.K. and J.R.N.: How do you view the role of architecture panning out in the future?

K.K.: Architecture has an increasing role to fulfill and can be compared to that of modern technology in that while the need for it grows, physically and

M2 Building, Tokyo, 1993. View from the road.

materially it disappears. In Greek times the architect was ahead of every other technology and in future this position must be regained with the architect taking precedence over virtual and computer technologies. The twentieth-century architect has only kept ahead in terms of civil and "material engineering" which is a very narrow field. The next century will be distinguished by architects who manage to combine various technologies with philosophy and psychology as well. Space as the basic matter for architecture is changing. Architecture no longer only deals with enclosed space or that of a city and its buildings but it also deals with psychological, virtual, or electronic space. I would highlight this as something we could call and approach as "pure" architecture.

Destroying Dichotomy

C.K. and J.R.N.: Although most of your work is outside Tokyo you have completed some projects there. It seems that strength as an architect in Tokyo is derived from creating something that stands as a monument to yourself and to the client. Your M2 building in Tokyo is really strong.

K.K.: In that building I tried to create a new type of strength, a chaos that contains a sense of being powerful.

C.K. and J.R.N.: You wrote that that building dealt mainly with a dichotomy of the capitalist world. You said: "I want to be the Piranesi of the electronic age" and "I will attempt to destroy twentieth-century capitalist dichotomy." This writing coincided with your feeling that architecture is in crisis. Did you feel that you needed strength and power to tackle this?

K.K.: I was referring to the crisis of "old" architecture, which relied on its materials, but we are already in a new era. I still insist upon using materials in an unhindered way and engaging various media—I am very free in my approach now. The important thing to mention in Piranesi's work is that he did not design real buildings: he used his imagination and translated that into architectural drawings and etchings. [Piranesi produced a series of imaginary prisons entitled *Prisons of Invention*

Noh Stage in the Forest, Toyama, 1997.

between 1745 and 1761; only one of his architectural projects was ever realized.]

New Definitions

C.K. and J.R.N.: In your work what significance does the term avant-garde have?

K.K.: I think that there is now an avant-garde of technology that might be thought of as the technology of consciousness. Looking at technology in only its material significance is now dated, and the technology of consciousness and of virtual things is today's avant-garde approach to this.

C.K. and J.R.N.: Do you envisage a future in which is there no architecture without philosophy?

K.K.: Yes, I think that philosophy and architecture must always be combined now that we live in an age where it's possible to do so. In the last century technology and architecture were separate entities. While computer technology has continued to develop, architectural technology has remained limited by its use of materials such as concrete and steel, so that

architecture was in essence left behind. In the next century we really ought to work on combining them.

C.K. and J.R.N.: In your architectural descriptions you use a vocabulary which sounds unfamiliar. You use words such as "particle-ization" and then place a different emphasis on familiar words such as "frames" and "filters": is this a device to shift the perception of architecture, changing our way of seeing it?

K.K.: Yes, that's what I want to do. If I use glass for example, I think of it as a kind of lens, which is quite a different approach to most architects who engage with it simply as a material. In Rafael Viñoly's architecture, for instance the Tokyo Conference Forum, glass is used as a material for sculpture. For me glass is the material of the lens, an optical device, glass is indeed just a filter between the world and the medium.

The Architect isn't God!

C.K. and J.R.N.: In one of your texts you say how important it is to be provocative as an architect. Is that really the case?

K.K.: Yes, of course. Only by being provocative can I become an architect. For the last fifty years architecture has been a provocative profession.

C.K. and J.R.N.: In the theater Noh Stage in the Forest in Miyagi prefecture, you intervened and changed the actual program of this project. Normally the architect is given a program with which to work from: do you think that architects themselves will come to decide programs in the future?

K.K.: In general I think that architects shouldn't make the programs by themselves, because the architect is not a god. That said, Osamu Ishiyama sometimes becomes a god!

C.K. and J.R.N.: It has been said in one newspaper article that you yourself are a rising superstar, and that you promote the idea of the architect engaging with all kinds of technology to create what you consider to be a personal approach. Isn't that characteristic of a superstar?

K.K.: But these ideas of merging technologies are not solely my own. I have friends in many fields—computer technology, sociology, psychology and philosophy—and I have discussed the future of architecture with all of them and all are against the old styles of architecture.

C.K. and J.R.N.: It is possible to trace similarities of approach in the work of Riken Yamamoto. Would you say that you and other former students of Hiroshi Hara can be identified as a group?

K.K.: Riken Yamamoto, Kyoshi Takeyama, and myself certainly belong to such a group.

C.K. and J.R.N.: Do you think that many famous Japanese architects can be divided into clear groups?

K.K.: Most definitely, I can distinguish Hiroshi Hara's group as I've described it, from the Kazuo Shinohara, Toyo Ito, Itsuko Hasegawa, and Kazuyo Sejima group and then there is Arata Isozaki's own school of thought.

C.K. and J.R.N.: Are these architects' concepts close to one another in any way?

K.K.: Kazuo Shinohara and Hiroshi Hara are quite different, but the students of Shinohara and Hara have recently developed some small similarities. Hara's students' goal was anti-monumentalism, using methods derived from studies of villages. For the Shinohara group the basic concept was that of abstract space, a very theoretical approach. The main idea of Shinohara is an "abstractness of space" and dematerialization, and making sense of that disappearance of material.

C.K. and J.R.N.: Shinohara and Ando are often considered to be the artistic architects of Japan. How do you feel about the notion of the "artistic architect"?

K.K.: This distinction between "art" and "no art" is not so important for me. Ito and Sejima learned about abstract space from Shinohara, but now they try to make their architecture into a more sociological issue, while Shinohara himself is not so interested in society. If you call one set of architects artistic you might easily call another group sociological architects.

C.K. and J.R.N.: In relation to the Hara group you mentioned the idea of village life. Can you talk about this?

K.K.: This is mainly related to ideas of anti-monumentalism. A further aspect of studies of the village is a sociological approach. When I studied sociological relations in Africa with Hara, I first looked at the relationships within a family and the roles of father and mother and so on, drawing a kind of plan of family relations. I then compared it with the shapes of houses and villages.

C.K. and J.R.N.: One of Riken Yamamoto's current theories is based around the social change that Japan is experiencing. Do you also sense a change in Japanese society today?

K.K.: Riken Yamamoto's belief, as I understand it, is that architecture can be a tool that can change people. I refuse to think like that. I think we can use every type of media to work together with architecture in the way that a family might, and also as an art. In opposition to Yamamoto's thinking, I don't believe that it is necessary for architecture to beat every other field. I have a more open and free approach.

Active Space

C.K. and J.R.N.: Apparently you are interested in the work of Bruno Taut and his thoughts on space. What do you feel about European or other Western architects' views on space?

K.K.: I think that European architects like Bruno Taut and Adolf Loos were trying to discover a new philosophy of space. Meanwhile American architects were concentrating on finding new styles and new shapes. These respective interests represent the crucial difference between the European and American architecture of today. I respect European architects such as Germany's Bruno Taut, Adolf Loos, and Mies van der Rohe in their search for a new space. Now other European architects, particularly those of Spain and Switzerland are developing in a similar direction, challenging ways of uncovering a new philosophy and a new lifestyle in architecture. Next summer I will go to Switzerland to see the buildings of Jacques Herzog, Pierre de Meuron, and Peter Zumthor: Zumthor is an especially interesting architect.

C.K. and J.R.N.: With regard to your own architecture, how do you see "space" and "program". Are they necessarily integrated?

K.K.: Space and the activity in the space are certainly interactive. The space that I create is derived from movement, it is not static space.

View from the Floor

C.K. and J.R.N.: Your office is situated near the rather grand offices of other prominent architects—Kisho Kurokawa and Kenzo Tange. Your office doesn't take up the entire floor of a skyscraper but is a rather modest wooden structure. Is this a comment on how you feel about your role or position in the architects' world? Is it perhaps a provocative statement?

K.K.: I always say that looking from a low position is very important for architecture. Tange always looks from high above but I think it is a good aspect of Japanese culture to see things from a very low position. After all in Japan we sit on the floor! Do you know the film *Tokyo Monogatari* [*Tokyo Stories*] by Ozu Yasujiro, a famous filmmaker in Japan of the 1950s and 1960s? What is interesting about this is that he made a special camera for filming from a very low position. In doing so he tried to change the sightline, to challenge the point of view. I have a special feeling for the floor: when sitting on the floor the body and the floor are always touching one another and therefore the floor becomes the most important element of architecture for me. We only touch the walls sometimes, but we are always tied to the floor.

Ryoji Suzuki

June 27, 1997

To reach Ryoji Suzuki's small office we passed through a small corridor those shelves were densely packed with art books and jazz records. Suzuki's wife had arranged a delicious lunch for guests and staff alike. The intense dialogue with the architect which followed resulted from these agreeable circumstances.

Brittle Edges

Christopher Knabe and Joerg Rainer Noennig: You seem to enjoy working with concrete and pushing its use to the limits, so that sometimes the concrete becomes quite brittle. What problems did you face with the concrete for your Azabu Edge building?

Ryoji Suzuki: There is a special technique for breaking stones in quarries and we approached this building's cantilever in a similar way. First we fixed the shape with drawings and marked a line where we would drill holes. Then we drilled along the outline of the shape, five centimeters in diameter, at intervals of thirty centimeters. Next we hammered the concrete down and that is basically how the shape was made. If we had simply hammered the stone down without those holes, which we tried at first, the final line would be too smooth and gentle. What we wanted was a really strong, harsh edge.

C.K. and J.R.N.: In parts the concrete is so weak it is breaking away. Was this an intentional process of dissolution in your work, in opposition to construction?

R.S.: Actually, when the building was under construction and the concrete was being laid there were a lot of pieces of concrete and steel fragments left at the construction site. I picked them up and exhibited them in a gallery in Ginza [a fashionable area of Tokyo]. In fact, I exhibited all the remains from the site. During construction a close friend of mine was taking pictures of Azabu Edge, so finally we had his pictures neatly displayed alongside my collection of debris from the building site.

C.K. and J.R.N.: Displaying the "remnants" or "off-cuts" from your building means that the building has, in a sense, moved. How does all of this relate to your definition of an architect's work?

R.S.: That's hard to answer. There exists a traditional world of architecture in which the completion of a building design is the extent of an architect's work. I don't think that has to be the case. The construction process itself can also be part of the architect's work. Depending on how you deal with the

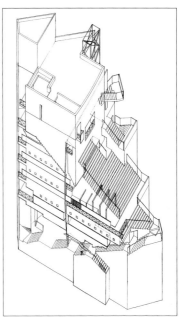

Azabu Edge, Tokyo, 1987. Above: west elevation; right: axonometric; below: hammered concrete cantilever.

building, the process of a building's transformation after completion may also be considered to lie within the realm of the architect. The architect might then be concerned with the building's state after completion, by this I mean its dilapidation, state of ruin, or destruction. If architects stop at the drawing board and no building is realized, then the parameters of their work might be that of the work of art. If you consider periods such as the Renaissance when painters were architects, you'll find that the buildings depicted in their paintings defined the architectural mainstream of that time. It was in fact their artworks that contained their ideas about architecture more than anything else. There are painters, Piero della Francesca for example, where it is difficult to tell if he was primarily a painter, an architect, or a sculptor. Even in the fifteenth and sixteenth centuries completing a building wasn't an architect's sole occupation, and the borderline was not sharply defined.

Computers Design Clones

C.K. and J.R.N.: In an age of digitalization there are new methods and new media for representing architecture. What media do you find most appropriate for expressing architecture?

R.S.: There are various methods of dealing with and making use of all this media; it is a field that has been extended enormously. At the same time the framework an architect sets for himself defines the limits of any possible usage. Media in terms of architectural representation seems to be limited to photography, essays, and drawings, but we should feel free to use other media for this kind of expression. The possibilities shouldn't be restricted; films might be one interesting way of displaying architecture. Many people are now aware that films occupy a very close position to architecture and that it could be a very powerful medium in architecture. It's just that no one has succeeded in that field so far.

C.K. and J.R.N.: Do you use computers at all or isn't that technology appropriate to your work?

R.S.: The computer is merely a tool so there is always some degree of use for it. But what most people do is exploit computer graphics to make their projects look gorgeous and exciting. What happens at the end of the day is that most find they have used their computers in the same manner and that their representations all look similar! If you simply look for effect, you end up with the same thing. The recent fashion is to work with 3-D images; this is easy, so everyone now illustrates their work in 3-D. What I want to do is to use computers in a different way. I should like to imagine what a computer really can't do and in what area it does not or should not specialize. I want to experiment in trying to make unnatural use of a tool such as the computer. I am also obsessed with trying to draw sketches as if they were printed out from a computer, as if the human hand were imitating the computer. I think it is more fascinating if you reverse the idea of the computer's use, but I find all this rather difficult to explain. For the Yokohama Sea Terminal competition drawings, the first sketches were naturally done by hand, but what I did was to add all the numeric data for the shape of the whale's curved back into the computer and obtain the final drawings by CAD. What is so good about CAD drawings? If you compare them with drawings by hand, they look rather dry and inhuman, and this interests me. The next step I took was to project those drawings done by CAD onto the studio wall, look at them and try to draw in a more dry and inhuman way than the computer, but by hand. So despite being my handiwork, the final drawings resemble computer graphics. Drawing computer graphics by hand and trying to surpass real computer graphics is one of my experiments.

C.K. and J.R.N.: Computers don't really challenge our way of seeing. Computer animation relies on the same visual assumptions that painting made five hundred years earlier, engaging the same line of sight that we are already accustomed to, and in the case of architecture leaves our visual perception of buildings the same. In that sense, film certainly has the edge in challenging ways of seeing.

R.S.: There are all these new tools that increase the possibilities of how ideas and buildings are represented, but that doesn't necessarily mean that ideas themselves will be altered.

C.K. and J.R.N.: But in photographs of your work the image and the buildings are distorted and occupy totally different realms, so aren't the architecture and its representation becoming one through the new media?

R.S.: There is a difference between what the real architecture is in itself and what can be seen in films or in photographs. From the late nineteenth century photographs became the popular medium for introducing architecture. This caused a decisive change in the way architecture was regarded. Since then it has been possible to experience architecture without actually visiting the place and seeing it in reality. Architecture started to circulate all over the world in this way. Architecture itself and architecture by means of representation were detached into two different objects. The fact is, they are not the same, and it is not possible to unite them. It is wrong to treat them as equal, and deceiving if you regard them as the same. I really think that it is more interesting if you treat them as two different categories. Nowadays you can use the photographic medium strategically and pretend that what is visible through this medium is the architecture itself. That is a very effective strategy to persuade and seduce people.

C.K. and J.R.N.: Many representations of architecture exist in various publications and it would be difficult to call any of them definitive. Do you think film is able to capture a somewhat fuller image?

Yokohama Sea Terminal, 1995. Competition entry model.

R.S.: I am firstly interested in films because I simply enjoy the images; I love films but not because they are needed to capture architecture in time and place. However it can be said that the time when the film industry was coming into its own coincided strangely with the moment when something new was needed to develop our ways of seeing. The art critic Susan Sontag said that with the approach of the twentieth century the world started to appreciate everything anew, and that everything up to that point, regardless of how dynamic the culture had been, was now being abandoned or even destroyed. The medium of film and photography came into fashion when it was necessary. The time needed that type of media to function as artwork itself in order to capture what was otherwise about to be lost. In terms of photography the conditions for its fruition were already in place from the Renaissance period; all that remained was for technical problems to be solved. Leonardo da Vinci had long since had the idea of photography and the camera so why did it take so long for the camera to be invented? Film took a little longer to become fully established and, like

photography, happened when history required that things be recorded in a yet another new way.

Italian Inclination

C.K. and J.R.N.: How do you place yourself and other Japanese architects in relation to the avant-garde?

R.S.: The real avant-garde only existed at the beginning of this century and we still haven't digested all of their ideas. I don't think that the brilliance of that time has been fully appreciated yet. The avant-garde movement was interrupted by political forces that arose at that time, so we still don't know all the ideas its proponents may have had in mind. I don't think the Japanese are avant-garde at all, but Le Corbusier and Mies van der Rohe were. We should look closely at Mies and the time after his emigration to the United States in the late 1930s. Mies's reputation changed at this time to one that had a more business-like approach to his commercial architecture. In looking for the avant-garde it's a case of looking back to Mies and back to the Italian architect

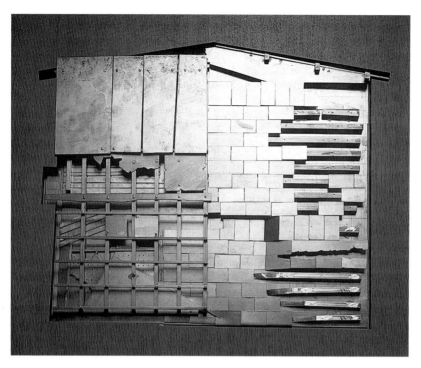

Barracks study.

Giuseppe Terragni, for example. Terragni was a fascist and his work was inevitably overlooked after the war until the architectural historian Manfredo Tafuri, amongst others, suddenly decided to promote him in the 1970s. Only now are we able to realize the significance of Terragni's work, but that said his work is still greatly underestimated. I think he might even have been greater than Le Corbusier.

C.K. and J.R.N.: You seem uncomfortable about being called avant-garde yourself, perhaps your position is better described as being "at the cutting edge". How do you know when your ideas are in such a heightened state?

R.S.: I don't, until it happens. It happens moment by moment, I just feel it and cannot explain because it is too difficult.

Barracks

C.K. and J.R.N.: Your work seems to illustrate some sort of tension between conservatism and the avant-garde, the buildings have a sense that something is lost and undecided about them. The buildings in

your barracks series demonstrate this tension and the idea of being "on the cutting edge". [The word "barracks" is used here in the sense of non-architect designed makeshift structures incorporating cheap materials such as the corrugated iron one quoted in Suzuki's designs.]

R.S.: I appreciate it if some critics say that this barracks work is "on the cutting edge", but I created it just because I was interested in the ideas I was discovering at the time. In the barracks designs I didn't intend to be avant-garde but rather more simply, I thought I'd hit on a good idea.

C.K. and J.R.N.: The barracks structures don't necessarily have your stamp on them; they might even be described as part of Tokyo architecture as the sense of your personality is understated and as "creator" your role is almost imperceptible.

R.S.: I was really not aware of being avant-garde when I worked on these barracks studies, or that my work might be thought of as Tokyo architecture but I agree that the work might have been created by processes that make up Tokyo city.

C.K. and J.R.N.: A lot of Tokyo is built by "designer" architects but are you more interested in the spaces between buildings, the voids, and this makeshift type of construction?

R.S.: Understanding these new spaces is something I'm really interested in and that's actually why I made the barracks models. I find this work fascinating but it takes a long time for me to define what it is that I'm trying to find out. I cannot always explain what the works are about straightaway—what I study is not intentional, or planned. I am less interested in explaining the spaces and more in finding out about them. It might seem that an architect's job is to put original ideas into practice, but this is not necessarily true, it is often the case that you are not aware of the work's meanings or implications at the time of their inception. Actually I think other architects share the same feelings about this. They might speak as if they have the greatest ideas, but most realize what they want to do much later on. There is always a question left behind which needs to be solved. Often an architect discovers something interesting accidentally and then wants to work on it. Then the job is to find out why it is so interesting. But the production of questions is rather more important than coming up with an answer or idea. Questions always throw up new interpretations for our work and I appreciate that, because it takes the work and the ideas further.

Forgotten Spaces

C.K. and J.R.N.: Traditionally architecture is a discipline bound to considerations of space. Your perception of space differs from that of the generally accepted notion of architectural space. You have taken up French terms such as, *clairière* [clearing], *creux* [hollow] and *vide* [gap] to circumscribe an alternative perception of space and challenge what you see as the limits of the word.

R.S.: What you can find out from any of these terms is important. Nowadays architects often use the term space. Its use became fashionable in criticism of the Baroque period, and it has remained popular throughout the nineteenth and twentieth centuries. The current use of the word "space" still includes something of the implicit Baroque meaning and for me is somewhat unclear and outmoded.

If I stuck to accepted definitions of space I really couldn't describe certain features. Space doesn't accommodate the sudden appearance of a void when a building is torn down; it doesn't reach the description of a cave without spatial undulations; and it cannot illustrate the emptiness that can appear right in the middle of a forest which I would call a *clairière*. The moment we stop using this term space as such, we suddenly start to realize different types of space that had been forgotten or marginalized.

C.K. and J.R.N.: You have previously described these new spaces as "eliminated spaces".

R.S.: That's right. Many types of space have been denied inclusion under the space umbrella, and gaps between buildings are a good example of those that have been ignored or eliminated.

C.K. and J.R.N.: In Tokyo these forgotten gaps are an almost representative feature and your work seems quite dependent on them. Are you inspired by Tokyo in particular?

R.S.: I'm flattered that you think I'm inspired by Tokyo, but this perception of space and these gaps are not limited to that city. When I look at Louis Kahn's work I feel the same sense of space running through all his architecture. In Kahn's Fisher House for example there is this awkward dead-end triangular space which cannot be properly grasped by the term space but he is obviously interested in this part of his design. If you look at the Baroque buildings in Germany, you will often find a staircase on one side and a hall on the other—an irregular space called a *Nische* [niche]. This niche was always painted black and was then eradicated from the plans, eliminated by structural usage. These gaps were filled with structural material that was deemed to be unworthy of presenting.

C.K. and J.R.N.: Are you more interested in exploring forgotten space than any designed space?

R.S.: Yes, I can't deny my curiosity about eliminated space, it exists in contradiction to traditional monumental spaces.

Nationwide Metropolis

C.K. and J.R.N.: You say these gaps aren't confined to Tokyo so it was logical that you pursued their exploration elsewhere. Do you think your Sagishima building implies a similar notion of space?

R.S.: I cannot tell how applicable this idea is or if it is applicable anywhere else. What I find out from one project is not intended to be applied to all future projects or even to the next one. To my mind the projects are all different. Going out and looking around to find out something else about space and to build something new is totally different for each project. In the case of the Sagishima building, Tokyo totally slipped out of my mind, because it was completely different from any Tokyo project as it was on the seashore. With the Sagishima design I considered the sea and the effects of sunlight entering the building from all directions, something we hardly ever experience in Tokyo. In Tokyo we build under various difficult and strict conditions and have to mold our concepts to accommodate these. In Sagishima, however, we were given a site free from tight restrictions for the first time. This meant that we could be more concerned with making the most of the site. I would disagree if you described the Sagishima project as Tokyo architecture.

C.K. and J.R.N.: It isn't Tokyo architecture but it does bear similarities to your city work inasmuch as it contains both cracks and gaps that are characteristic of your city work, whether by design or not.

R.S.: I did not strive to design the gaps, they just appeared because of structural problems. It was

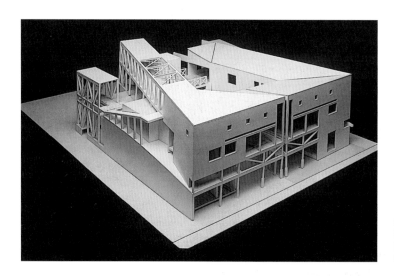

Sagishima "Ring" Guest House, Sagi Island, Hiroshima Prefecture, 1994. Left: model; below: light entering through glass slits.

Absolute Scene,
Tokyo, 1987.
Residence, scheduled for
demolition, is dismantled
down to the panes of glass.

quite a large wooden structure and we needed a lot
of columns to accompany the structural joints: plac-
ing the various rooms in between caused the gaps.
The building also has these narrow slits which let in
light, so one way or another and intentionally or not
you might say that I have a special sense for gaps!

C.K. and J.R.N.: How do the various conditions in
Japan, be it urban or rural, affect your architecture
in terms of its context?

R.S.: The conditions in Japan have to be differentiated from those in Europe. In Europe you have a
city and then nothing, a city and then nothing. In
Japan all the cities are connected and run into one
another. You have one city from Tokyo to Osaka or
even as far as Hiroshima. Japan is a nationwide
metropolis. There are houses everywhere so it's easy
to feel that you are still in the same place even
though you've just traveled across country, so in that
sense you might say that Tokyo is spread all over the
country.

Archeology

C.K. and J.R.N.: Your 1987 project entitled Absolute
Scene contains something archeological about its
conception. What benefits do you think an architect
can draw from archeology?

R.S.: Another hard question—ask Michel Foucault!
But seriously, archeology is a very interesting field
for architects, first because archeology is the opposite of architecture and second because it represents a
different way of looking at things. When you look at
something unknown you are generally wondering
"what is this?" and endeavoring to compare it with
something familiar. But in archeology you don't relate what you see to something you already know,
but start from the position of trying to find out something about an object which you have never seen
before. Instead of analyzing something within the
extent of the knowledge you already have, in archeological terms you have to approach architecture as

something that is, for the moment, outside your knowledge. What this means is that when you first perceive a building you stop describing it in familiar terms as, for example, a "commercial building" or as a "Postmodern design", nor do you say "I know where these windows come from". In place of these given points of reference, you start thinking more along the lines of "what a complex mass this is", asking what it might be, and noticing things about its surface and features. I think it is possible to bleach out old attitudes and take up new approaches by means of archeology. It is more a means of discovery than of invention.

C.K. and J.R.N.: Le Corbusier and Oscar Niemeyer always wanted to invent, so this discussion about an archeological approach seems to be a statement pointing towards the end of Modernism.

R.S.: You talk of Modernism but let's say avant-garde instead, that of the beginning of the twentieth century. If we analyze the architecture of that time with the same old architectural theories, it would seem extremely boring now. But if we throw those old ideas away and start off with a clean slate, looking at their architecture from this archeological viewpoint then their theories might still feel very exciting.

C.K. and J.R.N.: In your essay "Architecture of Specimens" you considered "escaping from a closed circuit" where the result and the input is fixed. Inside this circle there wouldn't be any problems, it would simply work. This escape seems possible as you attempt to break with the traditional scope of architecture in looking towards archeology. Can this escape also be found in your fascination with various media such as photography and movies?

R.S.: I'm simply interested in fields other than architecture, that's why I choose to talk about other topics at the same time. Relying on an established comprehension of architecture is restricting, so I look to areas that are generally considered to be non-architectural such as films, music, literature, and philosophy. Too narrow a field of reference often obstructs perspectives on architecture. I also think that it's important to take part in other fields, not merely being aware of them or standing by watching. Get involved, buy a camera, take pictures, and start shooting films! In that way I can find new interests or viewpoints and most importantly new questions. This way more interesting problems are raised and need solving. It is in fact these varied interests that leave me precious little time for planning: I am a poor architect!

Radical

C.K. and J.R.N.: Have you drawn the terms *clairière*, *creux*, and *vide* from fields outside architecture?

R.S.: That is hard to tell exactly, as I chose the three words with architecture in mind.

C.K. and J.R.N.: In your barracks discoveries you have mentioned non-human elements in architecture. In your architecture, would you link the notion of non-human—meaning "not over-designed"—, with architecture that lacks sense or reason?

R.S.: I do not consider my work to be either non-human or lacking in sense. The barracks are not architecture in that sense. The actual barracks themselves are independent from what I wanted to investigate through the designs and the two things really have to be considered separately. To design architecture right from the beginning is a totally different experience and a different way of working from constructing the material object. It most certainly isn't my intention to design architecture without sense or without any human considerations.

C.K. and J.R.N.: But the studies themselves could possibly be transformed into architecture and the barracks, as city architecture, appear to question the designer himself. Isn't this part of your radical questioning of space?

R.S.: This is something that other people say to criticize my work but again is not what I aimed for. I am not even sure if the ideas or designs could be thought of as radical.

C.K. and J.R.N.: Should an architect feel a sense of responsibility in relation to architecture such as yours?

R.S.: I am interested in these buildings but I'm not so concerned with responsibility. At present architecture is generally expected to be something practical or functional. In the past it was different: the space that Mies created in the Barcelona Pavilion for example was pretty difficult to use. It is not a practical building at all but what it does illustrate even today, are his universal ideas and his model for the world. In that sense I might gain some inspiration from these barracks later on.

Architect versus Client's Agenda

C.K. and J.R.N.: To ignore responsibilities might be essential in some cases but how about the clients? The owner of the Azabu Edge building wrote after completion: "I was in love with my architect but he went too far and I could not stop him. At the end it was hard, as he exceeded the budget threefold."

R.S.: I have never ignored my clients. Naturally clients vary and what they have in mind differs with each project. When you create real architecture you must always work together with the clients, engineers, and builders. Once you have started working together you find that you can really share your ideas, and then the clients don't necessarily want to limit the building to functions. The discussions in the design process might start off with functional arrangements, but you often end up sharing the same feelings towards the architecture. It is much easier to do this when you all pull together.

Small Group Charisma

C.K. and J.R.N.: Do you think of yourself as an enthusiastic worker?

R.S.: I am basically against the idea of enthusiasm as such. I think that the greatest failures of the twentieth century arose from enthusiasm, so I try not to get too submerged in my work. But having said that I do usually end up being enthusiastic about it! Being excited for its own sake is OK as an individual but not for a group—here I have fascism and communism in mind. There were people who developed those ideas before they were better thought out, and so they were established as ideologies. Once such ideas are applied enthusiastically in large groups they grow into some gigantic monster. I think that similar things happen now through the media and that's not good either. At the end of the day it is a problem

of critique and enthusiasm—both must be kept in balance somehow.

C.K. and J.R.N.: Your office is made up of a rather small group. Was this a conscious choice?

R.S.: There is probably a different working style for larger groups but I have not experienced it so far. If you aim to make projects in big offices with a hundred or so designers, you need to employ very different methods from those that I use. Successful results are seldom achieved by these large organizations. At the moment we work as a team of four or five people and it is simply a matter of organizing such a group. Max Weber studied teamwork and classified different forms of groups and he found out that in order to succeed in creative work, the ideal is a small group such as a sect. There must be several given conditions to this sect. The first condition is crucial and that is that the team should not suffer for economic reasons—the group should not find itself worrying about the budget. Second, the number of members should be limited in such a way that allows each person close contact with the next, and that each member's role and work is known to all. Between five and ten members might be a good number. The third condition is that sometimes they should accomplish a miracle—not frequently—but from time to time you need miracles to happen. Weber says that this maintains the charisma of the group. Weber stated that all these conditions need to be fulfilled to achieve creative work. My own feelings on the subject are that instead of conducting an orchestra with a hundred players, I would prefer to play in a quartet or quintet, even a jazz trio or a rock band with just four or five members. The exchange of ideas and feelings whilst playing in a more intimate group is a style that would best suit me.

C.K. and J.R.N.: And an important element might be improvisation?

R.S.: Yes, and combining different elements as I have discussed earlier. Sometimes I feel like painting, then I spend most of my time in the atelier, just painting and sleeping.

C.K. and J.R.N.: Like Corbusier—painting in the morning, designing in the afternoon, writing at night.

R.S.: This talk is becoming too grand—I'm not Leonardo da Vinci!

Fumihiko Maki

July 9, 1997

We had already met Fumihiko Maki once before in 1996 at the International Bauhaus Colloquium in Weimar, Germany. This second meeting took place in Maki's sober study and office. Throughout the interview Maki was very focused and efficient, thus revealing his thoroughly professional stance in all matters architectural.

At Harvard

Christopher Knabe and Joerg Rainer Noennig: Mr. Maki, it may be possible to draw a connection between you and Germany's Bauhaus University. You visited the "Techno-Fiction" conference there last year; wasn't Walter Gropius the dean of Harvard Architectural School shortly before you entered that university?

Fumihiko Maki: At the time when I was at Harvard we had three departments and one program and Gropius was not actually the dean, but the chairman of the architectural department. So it is true that there's a connection, but it is also correct that Gropius had already gone when I became a student. Then Jose Luis Sert took over the position of dean from Mr. Hudnut, as well as the chairmanship after Gropius. I was therefore a student of Jose Luis Sert and he was a disciple of Le Corbusier, so strictly speaking I was not directly in contact with Gropius.

C.K. and J.R.N.: However, while you were at Harvard did you detect any kind of German influence or thinking that might have remained?

F.M.: During the time I was there, I'm not so sure. The heads of the school must have felt it, but there was no strong discipline inherited from the Gropius era that continued at Harvard. It might have been felt amongst a few people, but then those people became rather a minority. A number of students who studied under Gropius became well known architects later in the 1950s and 1960s. As you know, Gropius formed The Architects Collaborative (TAC). Several partners of TAC had been students under Gropius at Harvard so his influence was obviously much stronger in offices and ateliers run by those people, but less so in Harvard after Sert took over. Sert himself was on a different track; he even invited Le Corbusier to design the new Carpenter Center for Visual Arts there.

C.K. and J.R.N.: What about your personal relationship to Gropius?

F.M.: I had no personal contact with him—I had known him a little through mutual friends but in fact that was all.

Spiral Building, Tokyo, 1985.
Left: detail of facade;
below: interior spiral.

C.K. and J.R.N.: So, which was the strongest influence on you?

F.M.: The influence must have been a very rational one. I am of course the product of a Japanese architectural school, the University of Tokyo, where Kenzo Tange was my mentor. In this respect I have had no direct connection to Gropius' teachings or his philosophy. His influence, broadly speaking, was in my earlier years through a very rational sort of design method and in problem solving, form-making, creating ideas, and in how to make a program.

In that sense I might be in a certain amount of debt to early twentieth-century developments in Europe.

The Bauhaus seems to be more interested in the integration of art in architecture in a way that situates architecture as merely one element in a much broader framework. In my years at Harvard the emphasis shifted from art to urbanism. Sert was definitely interested in this shift, although he himself was much more an artist than Gropius. But nonetheless, he did not stress this aspect or relationship too much in his teaching.

Tokyo Church of
Christ, 1995.
Left: exterior view;
below: interior view
of translucent facade.

Tangibility

C.K. and J.R.N.: Referring to the design process itself, you called buildings "unclear wholes containing clearly defined parts." Do you think that this relationship between the whole and the elements might be valid for urbanism as well?

F.M.: Yes. When I started to study architecture I thought of it as being more tangible, something that could be dissected into parts with individual functions which would have novel relations, and that you could construct the whole out of those parts in a very rational way. But as I wrote in certain articles several years ago, architecture for me is now becoming more intangible, more enigmatic. The parts and the whole are incapable of being separated. I became more interested in more vague, nebulous images. There were discussions in England in the 1960s and 1970s that addressed two ways of conceiving an entity: "clocks" versus "clouds". One was a very clear vision about the relationship of the parts to the whole. The other idea indicated the whole as not being the sum of the all parts, and that no matter how many parts you may add, it still wouldn't create the whole. Here the term "whole" is very crucial if you are trying to pinpoint what exactly it is, as it always eludes comprehension and remains unclear. Therefore at some point in the design process, we just have to understand that there is something a bit mysterious about what we are working on and also in what other people are doing.

C.K. and J.R.N.: Do you sometimes try to evoke this kind of uncertainty in your designs?

F.M.: Yes. Architecture is not philosophy and therefore I don't get too involved with linguistic games in my explanations. I pursue a more intuitive process, whilst recognizing that certain rational elements must be considered in architecture, at least more so than in art. We are dealing with a number of constraints: we have to know how buildings are to be put together, and without rationality they would just collapse. But when we are talking about images as such, then the rationale isn't as important. Many architects try to rationalize whatever they have done or are working on at present, but in general I don't hold with that approach since processes like that seem very tangible. It would be better to leave the products to be judged and evaluated by some other interested party. What other people have to say can be very revealing—they may well say something I have never thought of or expected.

Latent Influences in Design

C.K. and J.R.N.: It almost sounds as though you perceive art and architecture as bearing some similarities to one another. Do you feel there's an artistic vein in your work or do you also collaborate with artists?

F.M.: Yes, I do work with artists but only in certain areas. Actually, I collaborate with landscape architects, but not with artists *per se*. We only incorporate elements of art into buildings that I design and that's all. However when you are conceiving some forms there might also be latent influences from art. If I like the work of the artist Chillida and his imagination or forms, that appreciation might merge into my subconscious and someday without explanation it might come up in the process of my own sketching or building; this sort of thing can certainly happen. In that way any information I receive can be deposited in my "safe" or my "bank" from which I can extract whatever I want later.

C.K. and J.R.N.: It's easy to imagine that art could be a very important inspiration for your work. For you the rational aspect in the overall architectural design is merely the working out of the project, and deciding on "intention" never appears as rational work.

F.M.: It is not rational at all. This whole process of making architecture might include some rational answers, such as why you have done this or that, and why I have brought out this element, but it is only a part of a complex process. To try to explain the whole of this in a completely rational way doesn't work in my case. I can't explain all this and my position is this: why do I have to explain?

C.K. and J.R.N.: In your Yoshio Taniguchi essay you said that "the wellspring of an architect's ideas lies in the depth of his consciousness."

F.M.: Did I say that? Naturally you have to be conscious of the things in front of you, then you can start to construct something out of them. There is a certain consciousness or I would rather say "desire to express." Getting new ideas is at times mere coincidence; I can spend an entire month just pondering different ideas and quite often I don't even have to draw, I can simply draw in my mind. I reject many ideas generated in my head before they come out in a drawing or in models. What that means is that only through experience can you gain something. Making mistakes is part of this—making new mistakes that is—but certainly not repeating old ones.

Critical Processes

C.K. and J.R.N.: For someone like Mies van der Rohe architecture clearly expresses "the will of an epoch translated into space."

F.M.: Zeitgeist?—I rather enjoy this very uneven and very nebulous process of architecture. The only thing that seems important to me is to construct a firm rationale but to remember that in the end it may betray you and your design. Young people tend to await a blessing on their work which is understandable, but to me one of the most important things in architecture is how you continue your personal development. It is essential that you believe you are

Kaze-no-oka [Hill of the Winds]
Crematorium, Nakatsu City/ Kyushu, 1997.
Left: view to the north;
below: interior courtyard
covered with a sheet of water.

still able to develop yourself, even if people tell you that you can't anymore. And let's face it, that can happen quite often. In design you always have to have a critical mind and this takes precedence even over developing your rationale, or setting up some grand theory which you will be the only person to follow. Instead it is better to develop a critical mind in order to make certain judgments on both past and present projects. It is necessary to refine these skills so that they can be applied to whatever you are doing. After three years or so you begin to reap the benefits of your own critical ability, and what can be improved on is by then hopefully self-evident.

C.K. and J.R.N.: There is that profound phrase you wrote: "If architecture gives joy, it is because it enables one to see oneself in space and to discover one's physical being in relation to the external world." Would you say that architecture was an appropriate vehicle for self-discovery?

F.M.: Yes, this is true, especially since I wrote it! I also believe in a collective subconscious. Architecture is a social art and therefore not just for personal consumption, unless of course you spend your own money building for yourself. Of course your house could be private as well as being a social statement, for instance the house of Frank Gehry in Malibu, which is surely a statement about the society of its time.

Coming back to the issue of collective consciousness, the responsibility of architecture, or maybe that of art in general, is to expose a certain latent subconsciousness which exists in society. It is not as pretty as zeitgeist; it is a more latent desire. A means of expression is not simply limited to architects. I believe that in terms of architecture even lawyers or laborers possess at least a latent sense of desire. If your architecture is to stimulate people's feelings—again I'm not talking not about architects, critics, or historians now—then I think you have to reach out to the very heart of people who are not immediately part of your social or work spheres. The reason I say this is that I have recently completed a crematorium and there are many people who saw it and wanted to be cremated there! These people were not architects but members of the general public. Obviously people's relationship to this type of architecture is unique. To me this was very important: after all cremation happens only once in a lifetime, it's not like a restaurant you visit and want to go back to. That people reacted to the crematorium that I have designed is very moving since it evidently communicated something to them, and that doesn't happen so often.

C.K. and J.R.N.: Tokyo is a city of such accelerated architecture, it might be difficult for the subconscious to manifest itself. Is it possible to relate this to your work?

F.M.: Yes. You can't assume a latent subconsciousness in everything, only in certain cases. But through design you can at least raise critical questions for people. If you build a city on your own and offer some space to people, surely they will start to respond to this space and use it in some way. This is how I establish a link between myself and what other people are doing there. To me, testing architecture means not only pleasing a client right now, but also seeing if what you have done works socially. This is both the enjoyment I get and the sadness: if people begin to behave indifferently towards the work—which happens quite often in many of my buildings—I can feel quite disappointed. I can never quite weigh up which building will draw a more positive reaction and which won't. In the latter case I wonder why it didn't provoke a more favorable reaction, and then this becomes the basis of my own criticism of my work. Whatever reaction you experience might be

useful in one way or another in becoming the essence of your critical faculties.

Reinvention

C.K. and J.R.N.: You stated that architecture is a social art, and modern Japanese society has certainly undergone considerable change. Do the issues of social change affect your work?

F.M.: You can't say that every change in society—from those in the education system, in the political system, or those in the monetary system—are constantly impinging upon your mind, and that this is the basis for design work. Frankly speaking, our position is not equal to that of writers, who can absorb all these things and put them into their work. Instead we have very few possibilities of using all or any of that in design because you design a maximum of just three or four buildings a year. We can only extract certain elements that could be related to designing buildings. Nevertheless, buildings are quite often the sum of conventions; almost half of all buildings must be so. But I want to repeat that by having a critical mind, you might be able to reinvent some conventions. I believe that this is the faith you have to have as an architect.

C.K. and J.R.N.: Then your "architectural desire" is one that follows a path to refine such convictions, more than one of being radical or trying to invent something new?

F.M.: I don't try to invent too much but I am deeply interested in reinventing something that has fallen out of existence. Material things are governed by certain reasons for their existence that you have to understand. Through having a critical attitude you might be able to reinvent and be able to create something new at the same time.

Japan at Home and Abroad

C.K. and J.R.N.: As you have worked abroad extensively, let's widen the scope from Japan to the international scene. Do you feel that your design strategy can continue to be successful in conditions different from those in Japan?

Makuhari Conference Center, Tokyo, phase I 1989, phase II 1997. Above: exterior of phase II.

F.M.: Do I still want to extend my activities beyond Japan? I don't have so many years left and so I'm not really thinking in those terms [Maki is in his seventies]. Whenever I am asked to design a building outside Japan and if I am interested in the proposal, then I am very pleased to do it. I have had a few projects in Germany and in the United States, but I don't like to have too many at once because they are so exhausting. If you want to work abroad it requires several times more effort than working in your home country. In Japan I know all the contractors and consultants and it is easy to control the quality of the design.

C.K. and J.R.N.: Like one big family?

F.M.: Yes. At least the relationships have been established for long enough. But it is a new challenge to design overseas and today there is the concept of the global society. Testing ideas out in new places is very challenging too.

C.K. and J.R.N.: Having studied abroad you brought the knowledge you gained back to Japan and then you have brought your vast experience abroad.

F.M.: That seems to me to have been a very pleasant experience and I don't want to end it. Regardless of what you do whether at home or abroad, you have to establish yourself in a mutual process as a link between two parties. At the very least you have to have good relations with your clients. Quite often architects are so egocentric that they unnecessarily create

many enemies, and as a consequence they only work for that client once. Architects must be able to respect the ideas of other people. Some demands and requirements are made of me and are welcome; some ideas from democratic societies are ones I like very much. They are not all ideological but are just exercising power or trying to gain maximum profit or are marketing their own name, and that type of power I dislike.

C.K. and J.R.N.: What was your recent experience in Germany like?

F.M.: I had a very remarkable experience with the city of Düsseldorf. We were working on a project there and the clients were not so good. After the competition, they wanted us to change the original scheme and we didn't want to do that because it didn't seem good for the environment. But they forced us to do so and our contract was terminated at a certain point. We finished the documents for the planning permission and then the client gave these revised plans to the city, but the officials did not accept these because they were no longer the original scheme. I am going back to see the city administrators in Düsseldorf and we will present our case. I don't know what the outcome will be. It was very surprising to see how the city reacted to these changes. The whole experience is a new kind of culture shock for me.

Atsushi Kitagawara

July 14, 1997

Atsushi Kitagawara's former offices, where the interview took place, was located in an underground level of one of his residential buildings. Kitagawara's staff worked in a flat, almost windowless, cellar-like space. The conference room chosen for the interview was bleak and sober. On one side stood transparent boxes containing experimental designs.

Soft Architecture

Christopher Knabe and Joerg Rainer Noennig: In your writings you often refer to stage architecture. Is there any connection between these ideas and your Cloudy Spoon building, an apartment block on the outskirts of Tokyo which we visited yesterday? The building is still impressive although it is currently in a rather dilapidated state.

Atsushi Kitagawara: The clients concerned with Cloudy Spoon have problems with facility management and in maintaining the costs for running the building. They changed a lot in the building, and even removed some parts.

C.K. and J.R.N.: The "curtains" and "drapery", in particular, which you designed have completely disappeared. In this building, you could say there were distinctive "hard" and "soft" parts and, since the "curtains" are gone, the soft part is eliminated. Do you think your initial concept is still working?

A.K.: In the case of the screens and in terms of the structure of the soft parts, although they have

disappeared, both hard and soft elements are necessary for the complete architectural concept. Architecture is always composed of parts which disappear and others which do not, some which are static and some which are dynamic. As for the textile screens in Cloudy Spoon, I think they have to be renewed all the time. Material, color, or form might change, but all this needs to be renewed.

C.K. and J.R.N.: Can this be seen as choreography? In the theater both the stage set and the actor only experience glamour briefly; soon they age and after a while they are going to be removed from the stage.

A.K.: This is exactly my intention—that the very soft parts in that design can disappear.

Science versus Eroticism

C.K. and J.R.N.: Do your current ideas relate to those in your publications up to 1992, where you interpret

Above: Cloudy Spoon, Tokyo, 1988, view from the north-east.
Below: Rise Cinema Tokyo, 1986, cast aluminum exterior wall.

Tokyo as an illusive or imaginary stage character? Apparently your present office makes more use of visual layers such as louver or lightweight elements, and this is certainly something new by comparison with works included in earlier books. What do you feel is the nature of this change?

A.K.: Georges Bataille had the vision that the world is divided in two: a rational side, based on science, law, and efficiency, and a side characterized by sensual eroticism, or poetic feeling, and which is "in favor of death". Human beings, he believes are attracted to death; they take pleasure in enjoying this darker side even if they try to behave rationally. There is that kind of twin desire for light and darkness. I think the role of an architect is to bridge the gap, or to make a straight path between the scientific, rational being, and the opposite elements of eroticism and death.

C.K. and J.R.N.: In your texts you called this dualism "Darkness at Noon" or "Day and Darkness". It would be interesting to try to understand something of the dark and mystical side of reality.

A.K.: I've been exploring and experimenting with this all the time and I'll continue to pursue it. While designing the Rise Building, I was more interested in representing the world of darkness. I was much inclined towards that aspect of the world—something of my maniac side predominated, and I wanted to represent one view. But currently I've started to think that these two sides of light and dark should exist in a balance in my designs. There is a need to bridge the gap and create a relationship between them.

Avant-garde

C.K. and J.R.N.: In general architecture is not designed using irrational images but you make frequent reference to art and in particular to Surrealism, which alongside other avant-garde movements tried to express the irrational, or the unconscious side of the imagination. Is it possible, that in creating the Rise building there was an extreme shift in your architecture from the rational to the hidden, possibly towards the irrational?

A.K.: When I define avant-garde, I would determine it as a strategy to break up conventional methods and notions in order to create something new. Do you know the snake Ouroboros [the symbol of continuity and eternity] which bites its own tail? Throughout history the avant-garde ultimately becomes the classic, and in that sense history repeats itself, like the Ouroboros allegory. The avant-garde is not eternal, so I think that all of us who work creatively, in architecture or in other fields, need to be avant-garde all the time in order to innovate.

C.K. and J.R.N.: Perhaps the term avant-garde doesn't describe your work well enough. You pose artistic challenges which sometimes uncover knowledge that, you have said yourself, is very difficult to explain. In Arthur Rimbaud's letter, he writes about a piece of wood which one day awakens to discover that it is a violin. It doesn't know what's happened to it, but it has achieved something completely new. Could this change, from the piece of wood to a violin, represent an idea of a new potential reality?

A.K.: I think it is essential to have an imagination. This is a key word. When you say Rimbaud's piece of wood forms a metaphor beyond the piece itself, I think that this is the essence of modern art. Atsushi Miyagawa, the art critic, noted that in contemporary art it is crucial that the viewer's imagination be stimulated. Before contemporary art it was purely the artists' vision that was considered and how they expressed themselves. What they needed to do was to allow the viewer's imagination to exercise criticism. These days almost all architects have pieces of wood converted into violins, and it might well be said that we simply have too many violins. We need to go back to a more primitive state and say it is time to keep pieces of wood, not convert them into anything, and just maintain them as they are. It is necessary to take the essentials from natural, fundamental things—I call it primitive architecture. We should go back to the primitive aspects of architecture rather than adding lots of decorative elements to make elaborate architecture.

C.K. and J.R.N.: This might be understood through the images in your recent architecture. Now your buildings are mainly assembled around an inner space: this can be a sloping garden, stairs or glass covered areas, or a central microspace. Perhaps this inside is an essential part of the city you've discovered, which is itself different from the "normal" city.

You have made other contradictory statements about the city. At one point you claim: "The city is not streets, buildings, crowds, and freeways—it is just a metaphorical condition we call the city." Later you said: "We seriously underestimated the power and influence of the physical aspect of the city." Which is more important: the metaphorical condition or the physical aspect of the city?

A.K.: This is not contradictory to me, and I put both statements together in an edition of my collected projects. When I wrote these texts I regarded the city as having both a visible and invisible side. The invisible means information technologies and virtual reality which exist in an unseen form but are growing bigger and bigger year after year. The contrast is that "visible" pertains to existing space such as roads and buildings. We tend to underestimate visible things because of the enormous growth of the invisible. Here I want to say that it is high time to rethink physical space.

Metaphorical City

C.K. and J.R.N.: Where the part of the design determined as functional, becomes less like that in "Invincible 2," the irrationality of that huge frame is superior and the absence of a rational function gives way to a metaphorical interpretation. Similarly with the Cloudy Spoon, there is a highway, and there is the building which is materialized, but at the same time you devised these frames penetrating the building longitudinally and these parts are very empty. It is a dematerialized body and the frame in the backyard has nearly the same volume as the building itself. Can we think about that as a second virtual nature of the building, like a metaphor for the invisible city?

A.K.: In the case of the Cloudy Spoon, we worked on related things, the contrast between void and solid, the frame and the cubic, functional and nonfunctional elements. Contrast was placed in the foreground. This frame is like fighting against a huge city or to use a metaphor, a Japanese soldier fighting with a bamboo sword against an American soldier in World War II. In some ways this is cynical, a mad thing, since it is as if you know you're surely going to

"Invincible 2", Atsugi, 1992, the Supergrid.

die, but you do it anyway. It's like Don Quixote tilting against windmills, such fighting is merely gesture. And the name, "invincible", comes from the American warship, The Invincible. Previous to that I also designed "Invincible 1," though it isn't realized yet and is ten times larger than this one!

The Fatal Circle

C.K. and J.R.N.: You wrote about economics as a new kind of literature. This makes economics something of an elite subject to be incorporated through classical examples into architecture. Literature can rightly be termed a real art, but can economics be an art too?

A.K.: Economics translated into literature and literature translated into architecture? Economics as a subject has almost gone beyond economists' comprehension. To make economics interesting I need references from art and to interpret economics as art. Economics is very complex; it is not something straightforward and it is not just composed of fragments. Let's look at it in the same way as we

do literature, sensitively and carefully. Economics has strong connotations and is related to architecture by a common ground, by a common context.

C.K. and J.R.N.: You have stated that economics and technology in modern times occupy the internal private life. Economics has become intimately connected with psychological and spiritual matters, and for that reason it has become necessary to use literature to gain knowledge about this economic private life. Technology that has grown up outside of man, turns into a kind of inner technology. Are economics and technology now part of our private lives?

A.K.: Let's look at what Kojin Karatani has said about nuclear weapons. Before the age of nuclear weapons, we tended to look towards the future, but after the birth of nuclear weapons, we now tend to look back to the past. This change in mankind's vision coincides with the beginning of retrospection among architects. Arata Isozaki has created postmodern architecture by looking back and quoting from classical architecture, but making connections with contemporary architecture. In this sense the birth of nuclear weapons started to permeate the

Big Palette, Fukushima, 1998, view from southwest.

human psyche so to speak, and wasn't just a superficial affliction. Economics, technology and design— all have the same kind of contradiction. During the Cold War between the former Soviet Union and the United States nuclear weapons were aimed at both countries, but aiming at each other means they challenged the world itself. They had pistols aimed at their own heads. In that sense there was a deadly circle—maybe we can come back to that image of the snake again. When people acknowledged the danger of nuclear weapons, on a personal, or "inside" level, then we all demanded the reduction of nuclear weapons and nuclear power. But at the same time, in terms of ethics, we have to consider other modern phenomena, for example, the recent cloning of sheep. That may happen to humans at some stage, and what happens then to the literal or intellectual inside? You can take the DNA and duplicate Professor Ishiyama to create one thousand Professor Ishiyamas!

C.K. and J.R.N.: What a vision!

A.K.: But this is in essence another kind of war, destroying the "interior life" of human beings, crushing human nature and human individuality.

Electron Wind

C.K. and J.R.N.: Was your architecture affected by the changes brought about by the bubble economy?

A.K.: The economy goes up and down, but I don't think on that level. If you say the structural system of the economy has changed and the political system has turned socialist, then this would actually have effect on architecture and it would change. But the very superficial nature of the bubble going up and down won't change my methodology or philosophy.

C.K. and J.R.N.: One thing that was closely connected to the bubble economy was the exuberance of architectural expression. You called the city today "the space where the electron winds blow," something that can't be expressed through form or style. Does your recent work express this abstract city where the electron winds blow?

A.K.: When I mentioned the electron winds, I was talking about information technology and the society of radio, newspaper, TV, computers, and the Internet. Nowadays we constantly feed ourselves as

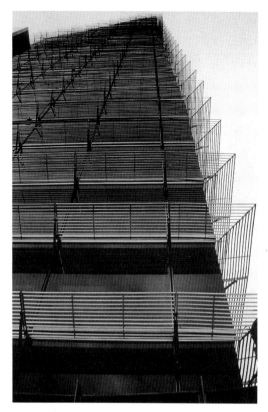

Above: Scala, Tokyo, 1992, south view. Right: Metrotour, Tokyo, 1989, view up the curtain wall.

much through modern media as through water or food and we might just die from this too.

C.K. and J.R.N.: Surely these electron winds are not something that could be expressed in design? You have quoted Jean Baudrillard and Georges Bataille, who said that expression arises from the "controlled look," the directed look. The controlled look is one that puts things in relation, "the path that cuts across the things...", it establishes meaning, it is not designed, it makes expression. Do you think it is necessary to make buildings expressive?

A.K.: I need expression. I set the following design theme at the university where I teach: "My Shape" or "My Form". The students had to express this through plans, designs, or models. I believe that the students have their own shapes, forms, or expressions in mind and this must come from their consciousness or ideas. Students in particular need to find the terms of their own consciousness level to translate it into expression. I don't mean

through decorative elements or ornament. They each have their own heartbeat and their own inherent individuality. Without that sense of individual expression or personality architecture wouldn't be architecture.

Expression is Everything

C.K. and J.R.N.: You have designed different kinds of architecture, not only in an expressionist style.

A.K.: To me every style is about Expressionism, even Minimalism.

C.K. and J.R.N.: At times your architecture contains elements of real color and brightness, like a stage set. These elements are even arranged dramatically, in such a way that the drama can change into a tragedy. Does this ambivalence mean that a sign can immediately change into its opposite?

A.K.: Yes that is my intention.

Metrotour, Tokyo, 1989.
The penthouse as a space for meditation.

C.K. and J.R.N.: Do some parts of your architecture intentionally refer to an idea of tragedy? For instance the "stairway to heaven" in your Metrotour building, or the "suicide jump board" in the Scala building? Are these examples of the change from the dramatic to the tragic?

A.K.: Yes, and each project contains different ideas and a different personality.

C.K. and J.R.N.: If we want to compare different kinds of Expressionism, we might say yours is a very personal type. German Expressionism has been very impersonal, it is more a social or public form. It was used to express the spirit of the epoch, the zeitgeist; it had little to do with personal matters. Your architecture seems to be a more personal one.

A.K.: Yes, my work is about individual expression, but in Japan itself this attitude varies. The big building companies such as Nikken Sekkei, for instance, have almost no personal expression and always tend to be very boring. Osamu Ishiyama's architecture on the other hand is very personal but liberal.

C.K. and J.R.N.: A recent critique noted that you form part of a group that is made up of vastly different architects, the group being Toyo Ito, Kazuyo Sejima, and yourself. Do you feel comfortable in this group? Do you think that this group shares any common ground or common attitudes towards architecture?

A.K.: Common ground? Toyo Ito tends to look up at the sky while he is walking in the street. He tends to look a little bit higher than directly in front of you. Sejima has very good posture and looks straight ahead, but I look down at the ground when I walk. I look below the horizontal line, and our office is below ground. I am what you might call introverted.

Itsuko Hasegawa

July 25, 1997

The interview with Itsuko Hasegawa took place in a house she had designed herself, while her atelier was located in another building nearby. Currently very busy with new commissions, Hasegawa managed to fit our interview in between two business meetings.

Homelessness and the Process City

Christopher Knabe and Joerg Rainer Noennig: In the magazine *Space Design* you discussed the issue of homelessness with the architectural critic Mr. Koji Taki.

Itsuko Hasegawa: Yes, I remember. We talked about it a lot.

C.K. and J.R.N.: Homelessness seems to have become a characteristic feature of Tokyo.

I.H.: At the schools where I teach, I often find issues concerning homeless people in students' projects. Under the elevated Japanese highways there are small vacant spaces and I advised the students to design dwellings for the homeless there. Despite finding the issue of homelessness examined in students' work, I can't recall architects being involved with this problem. When I had that conversation with Mr. Taki and mentioned the plight of homeless people in relation to architecture, he was surprised at first but later on his interest grew and he became more involved. I think of architecture in terms of the "hardware" of the buildings and structures on one hand, and the

"software" of peoples' movements and evanescent phenomena on the other. When you think about the cities of Japan, you deal not only with hardware but also with this software, especially in Tokyo. The problem of the homeless doesn't appear to be a short term one, it has become a matter of fact for this city. The Shinjuku homeless problem developed quite recently [Central Tokyo's Shinjuku station, often acts as temporary cover to the local homeless community], but I believe that this situation is also going to be long term. From now on architects will have to include this type of issue and consider population movement when they think about the city.

C.K. and J.R.N.: Mr. Taki stated that "the Japanese city is not an environment from which architecture can learn or mature" and that any building project in a Japanese city only results in "a kind of ruin." But the new conditions, including homeless people and city "software", provide crucial problems for architects to solve.

Homeless "box men", Shinjuku underground station, Tokyo, 1997.

I.H.: My point of view differs from that of Mr. Taki. He perceives Tokyo as something constructed out of particular buildings and city grids, and that it exists as kind of "hardware". My view of Tokyo however, is that of a "process city", forever changing and never finished. I think this is true of the relationship between skyscrapers and very small local houses that coexist in places such as Shinjuku [where traditional wooden structures still stand sandwiched between modern concrete high-rises that are constantly being demolished and replaced]. In the small-scale wooden houses, shops, or kiosks, you find that human relationships parallel the longevity of the structures they inhabit.

C.K. and J.R.N.: The coexistence of the homeless and the high-rises seems surprising. On their way to work, businessmen step over the homeless lying on the ground, and this appears to be another kind of accepted coexistence.

I.H.: They simply don't recognise class. You have to remember that we were influenced by American culture after World War II and by America's

education system and this classless theme was part of that. In Japan there is often no visible distinction between homeless people and the rest of the population: a homeless man might wear a smart suit and a businessman who's missed the last train, might well sleep in a cardboard box. It is not unheard of for a homeless person to become a white-collar worker, or for a businessman to become homeless. The businessman and the homeless certainly look very similar and both of them are symbols of a male society and of the economic society. It is possible that some of the homeless wear very nice clothes and go to eat at a fine hotel once a month and that white-collar workers sometimes lunch at the cheapest *yakitori* street stand.

Shanghai meets Hong Kong and Berlin

C.K. and J.R.N.: Architecture can change rapidly in a city like Tokyo, and this makes it a rich area for study with its extreme contrasts. Do you think the conditions prevailing in Tokyo can be found elsewhere and might even apply to Europe in the future?

I.H.: I have just returned from Shanghai in China. Incredibly high buildings are now under construction there where small houses used to stand. The original scene has now disappeared and they are trying to create a city like Hong Kong. As China is a communist country, the land is owned by the nation, possibly making it the richest nation of the world, and the people living there have to pay a kind of city or land tax. Nobody, not even private companies are allowed to own land. So the country holds a lot of power in controlling or changing the conditions for building. In that sense, it is still very different from Japan. In Shanghai there are two thousand four hundred buildings currently under construction. The architects there are bureaucrats and the ratio of architects to population is the smallest in the world. In China all the new structures are monumental and highly decorated like some Art Deco buildings in New York. When I returned to Tokyo, the city space seemed rather basic by comparison. Here in Tokyo, the architects are mainly motivated by the amount of

money invested, and that's all. If we now look at a city like Berlin, its style seems so conservative! Building design there is at a very low level. Nevertheless Berlin and Shanghai are comparable in the sense that both are currently undergoing a great deal of construction. These cities' conditions are however, entirely different. One is the German capital, the other is a communist city, and it is very clear that both are deeply influenced by their respective politics.

Communicated Architecture

C.K. and J.R.N.: The culture centers you've built— Sumida and Shonandai for example—articulate your response and sensitivity towards the people who will use them. This is a feature often lacking in the work of male architects.

I.H.: Shonandai was the first of my public buildings. I have spent ten years building social facilities and I think it is very clear that these have influenced a lot of other public building projects. Before the

Shonandai Cultural Center, Fujisawa, Kanagawa Prefecture, 1991.

Shonandai Cultural Center, 1991.

Sumida and Shonandai centers, public facilities used to be very conservative, but after their construction the situation changed rapidly. Buildings were affected not only in terms of style, but also in how they were used. In deciding upon a design method for the buildings, I had a lot of conversations with the clients and especially with the people who would be using the building, usually local people. Then I introduced the concept of "software." I not only influenced the form of the design, but also wanted to influence the stance of buildings in society.

C.K. and J.R.N.: Is it necessary to employ different forms of communication when talking with local people about these projects?

I.H.: In general I have very good communication with local people, and there's no particular reason why this shouldn't be the case. I get on well with people from all walks of life. I wonder if it is just a natural ability since many architects find it very difficult to talk with people, so they come to me and ask what kind of language I use. [Japanese makes use of many different honorific forms that are gender-, age-,

and class-specific.] In the countryside we use very different language from that in the city.

C.K. and J.R.N.: Once you wrote that "the most important thing in making architecture is listening."

I.H.: Yes, that's right!

C.K. and J.R.N.: Architecture somehow involves this art of communication.

I.H.: You can deal with architecture in a narrower or broader sense. Some regard it as a problem of engineering or a problem as an object to design. For me, since my early career, I believed architecture to be a more complex system, not only a matter of engineering or design. I have chosen a difficult course.

Working as a Team

C.K. and J.R.N.: Your work in the public sphere became a decisive turning point for your working strategies. Your earlier architecture was close to Shinohara's "zero degree architecture" in which one can detect a sense of indifference towards people.

I.H.: From the beginning, I maintained a certain distance from Shinohara and tried to do things differently from him. Even back in the 1970s when I was designing small houses, I wanted to open up architecture by communication, so this was already an important theme for me. In that way, there's been continuity in the development of my design, and my approach to house design is applicable to any building. I introduced that method into designs for public facilities, and this is perhaps the main difference between my work and that of other architects.

C.K. and J.R.N.: With regard to your public architecture you stated that you just want to offer a "suggestion of space." The Shonandai center has a big variety of spaces and the building still seems to be in a state of incompleteness. Is that your intention?

I.H.: While I was working on houses I tried to collaborate with other people. It wasn't just my own work, and I think that this creates an atmosphere free of restrictions—a building in which its functions are given priority.

C.K. and J.R.N.: The Shinohara school of architecture avoids dealing with the inhabitants.

I.H.: There is a very famous theory by Shinohara called "Houses are Art" written about thirty years

Sumida Culture Factory, Tokyo, 1994.
Left: aerial view; below: interior.

ago. Every time I meet him, Shinohara uses "I" and "I am", he never says "we" and this is very similar to these young architects who are practising his theory to the letter. On the contrary, I always say "we."

Artificial Nature

C.K. and J.R.N.: Your architecture plays with motifs drawn from nature. Can you talk about this?

I.H.: When Japanese people talk about the body or about their feelings and about being comfortable or relaxed in some way, it is always in relation to nature and never about technology. What we have to do now is to clarify whether we are faced with a new type of nature. Originally, the term "nature" referred to people's living environment. In cities in particular, we now live within completely man-made environments, so we have to deal with that kind of environment as a new "nature."

Hajime Yatsuka

August 5, 1997

Hajime Yatsuka is well known for combining his design practice with prolific work as a writer, theorist, and historian. Yatsuka seemed well prepared for the interview, introducing books, magazines, and his own design works into what became an encyclopedic conversation.

Theory in Action

Christopher Knabe and Joerg Rainer Noennig: Do you think that a city of such heterogeneous elements as Tokyo slips out of the general field of architecture?

Hajime Yatsuka: Yes, I do.

C.K. and J.R.N.: Both your theoretical and practical works seem to transcend the accepted view of architecture. Do you aim to revise or freshen up some elements of architecture?

H.Y.: I think that refreshing some old aspects of architecture can have an effect on at least a small part of a vast phenomenon. We are losing a lot of the more traditional architects but I am trying to expand this decreasing territory.

C.K. and J.R.N.: Your combined concerns as both a theoretical and practical architect make you unique in Japan, because in Japan there is a high emphasis on the practical and engineering side of architecture. In America architects such as you are more common.

H.Y.: I think that there are some difficulties in arguing about theory because I have a feeling that in

America in particular, theory is something which is only pursued in the studios of universities or in the architectural press, and therefore it is only regarded in a rather narrow sense of the word.

C.K. and J.R.N.: In the case of America, then, do you see theory predominantly as a laboratory concern?

H.Y.: Yes, and it seldom goes beyond those small laboratory environments. I don't know if this is a good or a bad thing but the Japanese work at keeping directly in touch with social reality. We have to modify the scope of theory, but in a system of unity that is available to all and that is valid for a small community. I have never been a faculty member of any university and refuse to do so because I have no interest in academic studies. I have been trying to engage what you call my theory, while always reflecting on the social realities. This is a significant difference from the work of my Western colleagues. In the last twenty years I have had the feeling that the Western avant-garde has changed a lot and in the

1970s they had lost contact with social reality, focusing on their works in studios in universities, and in the architectural press. That kind of theory seems to me like a work suspended in the air, and renders contact with the "ground" or "air" of reality, absurd.

C.K. and J.R.N.: In refusing to work in an academic style, how do you relate theory to realization outside education establishments?

H.Y.: Realization is just one aspect of the reality of architecture. I have never neglected the significance of unbuilt projects, but in order to evaluate them, and to see the possibilities and limitations of projects, it is important to consider both the built and unbuilt. I was working as a coordinator for the so-called "Follies projects" for the Expo in Osaka in 1990. There I had a very good opportunity to become acquainted with and work alongside Western colleagues such as Daniel Libeskind, Peter Wilson, Zaha Hadid and Co-op Himmelblau. This was an exceptional opportunity for me to see both their theoretical and practical work. The Expo Follies were built to stand for a period of six months so this was a great opportunity for less serious and more experimental works.

C.K. and J.R.N.: Does this type of architecture indicate a break between society and the economy, perhaps creating works that lack meaning?

H.Y.: I think there are two ways of interpreting the work. You can certainly interpret the Follies as examples of a rather egocentric presentation. The Follies can also be seen as the first occasion to show people other possibilities for the environment and for design, illustrating something beyond the narrow-minded designs of architects.

C.K. and J.R.N.: As you have chosen to work between the fields of theory, practice, and management, do you feel that there is a general lack of theoretical concern in the current Japanese architectural scene?

H.Y.: I am exploring ways of broadening the front and restructuring conventions. This takes a lot of time and it is a pity that I only can find a very small number of architects who are interested in pursuing these goals. Most of them are only concerned with architecture in a very literal sense, as if architecture dominates the whole social scene.

Folly Fever

H.Y.: Following the Osaka Expo, Arata Isozaki acted as commissioner for the *Machi no Kao* [*Face of the Town*] project in Toyama prefecture: this was a second series of follies. With Isozaki I became a director for the Kumamoto Art Polis [a series of design projects undertaken in various regions]. We had two international symposia and expositions, one for the first stage in 1992 and the second for stage two in 1996. For the first stage we tried to invite large national projects such as the Berlin International Bauausstellung (IBA), the Frankfurt Waterfront project and the Barcelona Olympics project which are all quite different from our Kumamoto project. These European projects were chosen politically because we had to encourage the interest of the Kumamoto people and obviously the governor must have felt flattered to be associated with these large-scale concerns in Europe. The German architect, Wilhelm Klauser, said that Kumamoto Art Polis was also initiated as a strategy to infect the region with a new kind of architecture from the outside. He compared it with US Commodore Perry coming to Japan [1854] and carrying an infection here from the West.

C.K. and J.R.N.: It seems significant in both the projects in Toyama and the Kumamoto Art Polis that you explored ways of designing, producing, and promoting very small architecture. Are these small buildings a way of "infecting" a city?

H.Y.: Perhaps we could say they are a way of "stimulating" the city. The project that I have just finished is my second folly since 1990. It's for a national park in Niigata prefecture. A folly is of course relatively free in terms of definition and Japanese people are usually interested in something new and so welcome the idea. The folly could be a very good pretext for broadening the scope of what is called environmental design in the conventional sense. The 1990 Expo was a good starting point with very good examples of follies.

New Terms

C.K. and J.R.N.: Do you think that it is it now appropriate to use the term "architectural producer" as a new description for the architectural profession?

H.Y.: Yes, in relation to a folly project of mine, I even tried to show the government that the term "folly" could represent a new repertoire, or a new vocabulary. I then tried to explain that "folly" could be interpreted as a type of intervention and is a notion that can be expanded. I was later consulted by the prefectural government of Aomori who became interested in these ideas.

C.K. and J.R.N.: Do they now want you to pursue a project in Aomori?

H.Y.: Yes. Recently prehistoric relics were discovered in the area and they are now building a park in which to preserve them. Next to the park they plan to build a series of cultural and municipal facilities including a fine arts museum, an auditorium, and a research center for the relics. They want me to act as coordinator for the entire national park. The master plan is not terribly rigid, it is more flexible and responsive. What they require is something in the order of "master programmer" as opposed to a "master planner." The role includes responsibility for the landscape as a whole and negotiation with the various architects involved in the individual buildings. The intention is to create a serious dialogue between the environment, the buildings, and their programs. Of course the repertoire holds the possibility of addressing landscape design, follies, and new ideas about public art and presentation.

Consumer Society

C.K. and J.R.N.: Can you talk about the state of architecture in Japan at the end of the 1970s, leading into the dramatic changes at the end of the 1980s?

H.Y.: This ten year period was marked by drastic economic growth and commercialization, and this reality was reflected in the architectural work of the time, particularly in the field of commercial architecture. Some of the most important architectural achievements in the last fifteen years have been in the field of commercial architecture. I don't think of that in a negative light because my own work at the time was in that very field, and it was connected with the idea of the "desire of the people". People's

desire is quite a natural phenomenon in that kind of affluent society. The "desire of the people" created a very important revival of the cultural issues of the twentieth century. Mass culture, regardless of whether people think it is good or bad, was the most significant invention of the twentieth century. It was discussed by important critics—Walter Benjamin for example—who was very sensitive to the regulation of desire which was fostered by the rapid growth of the consumer society. In the 1980s we were more interested in the excitement centered around the rapid changes in society, and this was reflected in the architecture. At that time I became more and more interested in the institutional aspect of architecture which was motivated by my previous research projects for the Kumamoto Art Polis. For those projects I was faced with dealing with the conventions of bureaucracy and very delicate issues of local social conditions. In the 1980s individual architects didn't have any contact with the public and neither were they invited to work on public architecture, as this was monopolized by large commercial firms such as Nikken Sekkei or established architects such as Arata Isozaki or Kisho Kurokawa. Younger architects were certainly not given the chance to get involved in that field. After 1985 or so, a younger generation of architects was gradually given the chance to work in that sphere and the public authorities became more interested in open competitions for public buildings. The competition to design the Shonandai Cultural Center [Fujisawa, 1989] was won and built by Itsuko Hasegawa and this serves as a good example of the shift in attitude. The Mayor showed that he was open to commissioning a young and very talented architect.

Millennium Kingdom

C.K. and J.R.N.: In your texts you site the shift in Japan from a post-ideal condition towards one of complacency.

H.Y.: In the 1950s people—whether they were architects, politicians, or the general public—sought some kind of image of democracy for their society to assume. A typical example of this was the Peace Center in Hiroshima that was designed by Kenzo

Tange. The principal layout was very similar to his pre-war project, which was built ironically for the Japanese military government. Later in the 1960s people gradually came to lose interest in ideals and this was fed by the growth of national income; a sense of satisfaction set in among Japanese people as a whole. In fact the more they became satisfied with what was now the reality of economic strength, the less they were interested in ideals.

C.K. and J.R.N.: In your writing you also say that "democratic style" becomes a cliché throughout the world.

H.Y.: That's right and I have recently been writing a series of articles on this topic for *10+1* magazine. The central theme is what I call the "millennium kingdom." Although that title has nothing to do with the idea of Christianity I have borrowed it with that in mind, referring to the idea of a utopia, which is somehow similar but of course not the same. It is not the actual duration of time that is important to this kingdom but time as it is inscribed in people's minds. You can call it the "post-historical" modern city. In this millennium kingdom utopia finds itself alienated: there are no ideals and everything is simply fake. There couldn't be an ideal form of public architecture. For me these expositions as well as the theme parks, which are very popular in Japan, are the key to showcasing a millennium kingdom state. For both local events and large-scale expositions, the emphasis has shifted from theoretical experiments to a future of more image-oriented buildings.

C.K. and J.R.N.: Can it be said that in the 1970s there was the manifestation of engineering's relationship to technology, and that now there has been a further shift in emphasis?

H.Y.: Yes, from technology to image. Now everything takes the cue from images.

C.K. and J.R.N.: What is the most prominent concern of the millennium kingdom?

H.Y.: The most definite aspect of this millennium kingdom is that it is not confined within the exceptional environment of organized events or expositions such as the theme parks, but is concerned with evaluating all aspects of society as a whole. The book entitled *Disguising Japan* and subtitled *Disneyland-izations of the Public Buildings*, contains research by

the associate professor of Kyoto Kosen University, Mr. Nakagawa. Kitsch architecture could previously only be found on the roadside in Los Angeles, and was not generally considered to be architecture anyway. Nowadays these types of building are to be found as the prevailing form of public building all over Japan.

C.K. and J.R.N.: But previously you've said that what the American architect Robert Venturi meant by kitsch was different from that which can be seen in Japan.

H.Y.: Venturi's analysis and research was done at a time when it was necessary to criticize the stereotype of modern architectural discipline. But Venturi himself lost that particular critical disposition and became absorbed by the consumer society, in my view.

C.K. and J.R.N.: You talk of a post-ideal society and the end of history. Can you discuss how this relates to this new preoccupation with images?

H.Y.: In a society which is motivated by the progress view of history, a sense of right and wrong pervades, but once people realize that such thinking has only been a stage in history, they also realize that this stage, this time, has already elapsed. As progress was the decisive element of that period, and as that period has ceased, it follows that the progress of history also ceases. It also implies that there could not be any specific direction to follow next. What we are left with is a situation in which everything is possible and everything is acceptable, and acceptability is simply created by people's taste. In Japan we now have the culture of newness or what Ryoji Suzuki calls "newness culture." At the same time we have no definite values since these originated from history or tradition which is now gone, and in that sense the "old" has disappeared. This presents a serious situation, and for the serious architect there are perhaps two ways of responding to it. One is simply to present their own ideals and to call them into a state of critical intervention in the general situation. The second approach—or rather my way—is different and involves being more strategic: merely showing that something is different is not enough. We should change the paradigm and the convention as a whole, and for this we should work beyond the narrow territory of the architect in the classical sense.

Multimedia

C.K. and J.R.N.: Can you tell us about the multimedia center you were commissioned to design?

H.Y.: I was commissioned last year [1996] in February and the design had to be finished by October. I only had eight months in which I had to decide all the programs and finish all the designs. I acted as a planner in formulating the program and then got on with designing as an architect usually would. Then on top of that I was coordinating the pieces to be exhibited in the media-works gallery. Only yesterday I had a meeting to introduce various artists and media artists.

C.K. and J.R.N.: What kind of elements did you think such a media center should incorporate?

H.Y.: I proposed various kinds of cultural facility and a computer center to gather all kinds of information and administrative services. Let me describe something of the design. The computer center has no facade: it is just a black box, and it has a moving panel which lets in sunlight from the west. There is a theater which is open to the lobby but can be shut off by a screen. There is also a gallery and a media library. On the third floor is what we call a workshop in which the public can touch the machines that operate various elements within the center. Then there are the studios and it is at this point that the normal work of an architect stops—but here I started to act as coordinator for the exhibition. It was requested that we try to relate the activity of the facility to social considerations, and that these should be modified in positive ways. Let's take a special form of Japanese dance as a metaphor to illustrate this. There is a type of avant-garde dance called *butoh* and it is unique since it involves almost no movement, only very slow movements, in contrast to Western dances which are based predominantly on moving in some more active way. For the *butoh* performer, dance is more an artistic expression of the individual artist, and his desire or ambition is to relate this experience as an artist. Most people's appreciation of their own bodies is dominated by their conventional attitudes towards their bodies and what you might call "conventional use". This conventional use also includes what people expose their bodies to, through furniture for example, because the way in which a body relates to chairs forms part of how a person understands their body. Relating this now to architecture, what we wanted at the center was a media program that could accommodate the possibilities of specific media whilst being aware of the alternatives, similar to the way in which *butoh* suggests an alternative view and exploration of dance and of the use of the body.

C.K. and J.R.N.: Was this special sensibility towards alternative uses for spaces, and a fresh awareness of the body's reactions to these of interest to all of the design participants?

H.Y.: For this particular facility I was acting as planner, architect, and coordinator of the exhibitions. But unfortunately, I am sorry to say that most of my colleagues are not interested in those special aspects of the facility. For them architectural space is everything, and whether it is a good facility or not is not of their concern.

C.K. and J.R.N.: There seems to be some similarity between your concerns and those of Itsuko Hasegawa, particularly in how she prescribes the use of her buildings. She has on occasion gone so far as to introduce some training in how to use the structure. Do you think there are parallels in both your works?

H.Y.: She is more popular than I am but perhaps her main concern and mine are similar. That said, I am much more interested in the institutional side of architecture and she is more interested in the practical side.

C.K. and J.R.N.: You have explained your multiple roles in the media center. But when an architect intervenes on so many levels doesn't that begin to deny the public the opportunity for appealing to and engaging with their own imaginative response?

H.Y.: With reference again to Itsuko Hasegawa, her concern is in how to facilitate the activity of people, which is still based on present convention. In opposition to that idea I want to improve or renovate the conventions themselves. That is quite a significant difference between us. There is a pamphlet entitled "Reinventing the Body" produced by the architect Jun Aoki, the *butoh* dancer I have mentioned, and myself. It explains the ideas of the group we have formed. We are interested in conceptual psychology and the "Theory of Affordance"—this is the special interest of a professor at Tokyo University

Ten Chi Chin Folly, Nagaoka, 1998. Above: general view; below: inner space with glass path.

and was advocated by the American psychologist James Gibson. The theory is a drastically new interpretation of the relationship of creatures to the environment. The group also includes two media artists, a commercial planner, and a computer specialist, and all the members are submerged in the search for new possibilities surrounding the human body. We are interested in the body's relation to space, its relation with various media and with virtual reality.

Ten Chi Chin

C.K. and J.R.N.: Do you think that when virtual reality is presented just as sets of images it is bankrupt?

H.Y.: Yes. We believe the general interest in virtual reality is too confined, existing across a very narrow range, and isn't necessarily geared to the exploration of new possibilities. Virtual reality cannot reach the potential of the human body and human perception. This line of research and thinking that

we've developed is called the "Folly of Ten Chi Chin,"—*ten* means heaven, *chi* is the earth, and *chin* is humans: this is a very old traditional principle in the early composition of Japan. *Ten chi chin* represents a harmony in each syllable and flows with a natural continuity in the way that "one, two, and three" and "mother, father, and child" do.

C.K. and J.R.N.: Could you explain how this way of thinking operates in your architecture, in the actual Ten Chi Chin Folly itself perhaps?

H.Y.: The essential part of it is wood, then it has the "Miesian skyscrapers" which are obviously designed with Mies van der Rohe's notion of space in mind. The glass in the structure changes from mirrors to being semi-translucent and finally translucent. The site that it is built on was originally home to a small castle that was destroyed in the war. There is the tragic legend of a very beautiful princess who committed suicide at this place, so in one sense the folly is considered to be a funeral monument to her. The first "horizon" is treated as what we call *hashigakari* in the Noh theater plays and is the entrance and exit for the actors. The Noh stage is rather like a bridge, and in the folly this is designed only in modern materials such as metal, glass, and tiles. The roof is a very important part of this design and is treated as a second horizon; this is intended to ascend conceptually and infinitely. In that region there are a lot of prehistoric artifacts and as these reflect both the traditions and materials of the region, I have tried to incorporate the image of the earth, art, and the ground. The human element is represented mostly by wood but the public cannot go inside the folly. The floor is a grid and so semi-translucent, I conceived it as a stage for the *butoh* dancer, for the slow performance, a "performance in the air" if you like. The conditions for *butoh* performance are totally different from those of other types of stage, and the dancer is very excited about performing there.

C.K. and J.R.N.: Your theories attempt to be very far-reaching or all encompassing.

H.Y.: But there are problems that concern me. Perhaps my idea is too scattered, but what I am trying to do is to expand my scope in the established fields of planning, theory, and administration.

Competition

H.Y.: The Ten Chi Chin Folly is actually a revision of my competition entry for the Niigata Cultural Center [1992]. Interestingly Itsuko Hasegawa won that competition and it is now under construction. I liked my competition entry very much and this particular competition was a great opportunity for me, but I lost and only got second prize. (Laughing) It was a great shock and took me several years to recover!

C.K. and J.R.N.: Albeit Japanese in concept, your composition resembles the Lenin Institute by the Russian architect, Ivan Leonidov.

H.Y.: Obviously!

C.K. and J.R.N.: Do you make obvious reference to Leonidov's work?

H.Y.: I'm interested in Russian avant-garde architecture as a whole and Leonidov is my hero.

C.K. and J.R.N.: Do such similarities ever become problematic?

H.Y.: Hasegawa's winning entry in the Niigata competition is very similar to the Congrex project by Rem Koolhaas in Lille and both are connected to elevated walkways. I was very unhappy to see that, especially since both Hasegawa and Koolhaas were amongst my closest friends. After that it became difficult for me to maintain the friendship with Hasegawa because there were so many people talking about the similarities between the two projects. No one mentioned it in the public press, so I felt that I had to do that myself—not to defend any project of my own but to make the issues involved clear to the public. Since then I lost her friendship and that's a pity. Hasegawa and I were also among the six finalists for the Shonandai center competition, which she finally won; but I didn't feel frustrated and just congratulated her.

C.K. and J.R.N.: Are you happy to continue taking part in competitions?

H.Y.: Following the Sendai Mediathèque competition in 1996, which was won by Toyo Ito, I stopped taking part in competitions. Competition work is far too exhausting and this kind of small office is neither financially nor mentally able to do that often. If a winning competition project is very good I have no objection to it. But the Sendai Mediathèque competition and the Yokohama Ferry

Niigata Performing Arts Center
competition entry, 1992, model.

Terminal competition seemed to me to have turned competitions into a sort of a game. My impression is that the two winners, Toyo Ito and Spanish architect Alejandro Zaera-Polo, are very good at finding the solution.

Nonconformist

C.K. and J.R.N.: You have never spent very long abroad. For that reason do you think of yourself as a domestic or regional architect?

H.Y.: I am not sure. I have never lived abroad and indeed the longest I've stayed abroad was for four months—that was in Los Angeles. I was working for the Museum of Contemporary Art (MoCA) for Arata Isozaki. I worked as one of the six on the advisory committee for the forthcoming MoCA exhibition "The End of the Century," and wrote an essay on regionalism for the accompanying catalogue. Writing such an essay might provide an answer to your question. I was assigned the subject of regionalism by the museum simply because I was the only Asian involved in the advisory committee. I enjoyed writing, but I had never considered myself to be regionalist at all. Since I had been interested in studying the history of modern Western architecture, I had thought myself to be a very hard-core modernist. But during the last six years while I have been working

for the Kumamoto Art Polis project, my basic feeling has changed a little. I wouldn't call myself a regionalist architect in the normal sense of the word, but I began to feel a sense of nonconformity or difference, especially while I was talking with people such as Rem Koolhaas who is both a modernist and an internationalist. In spite of Koolhaas's interest in cities, the regional problem or small problems aren't really matters that concern him. I am interested in issues both large and small and my article on regionalism is a critique of the so-called "critical regionalism". I don't want to deny the modernists' view nor do I think that it is merely a reaction to regionalism, but for me regionalism doesn't exist any more in contemporary society. Furthermore I don't believe that internationalism exists any longer either and certainly not in a pure form. Kenneth Frampton and Alex Zondersfolt claim that critical regionalism is ultimately critical internationalism. If critical regionalism and critical internationalism are the same thing it means there is no discrepancy between regionalism and internationalism and this seems problematic to me. "Critical" as a prefix is something that is very hard to define or follow through.

C.K. and J.R.N.: And the concept of the Kumamoto Art Polis can't be considered as regional since you invited architects from all over Japan.

H.Y.: It is neither regional, nor national, nor international—it is just contemporary.

Hiroshi Hara

August 8, 1997

In the interview room the walls were densely covered with photographs and fragments of text from a forthcoming book. Through an open slit in the ceiling we could hear people working. Hara came in and guided us to a large table on the elevated platform in the center of the office.

The Hara School

Christopher Knabe and Joerg Rainer Noennig: Some architects, namely Kazuhiro Kojima, Kengo Kuma, and Riken Yamamoto, have referred directly to your educational methods and the Hara School. How would you describe your ideas of teaching and the specific character of your methods at Tokyo University?

Hiroshi Hara: I don't think of these different architects as one school. Nevertheless, I do feel that we share something like the same attitude. There might be common concepts or one basic language.

C.K. and J.R.N.: How would you define that common language or vocabulary?

H.H.: We have been researching the notions of "city" and "communal spaces", it is mainly from this, that we have derived our common themes and vocabulary. We are trying to establish a relationship between settlement spaces and the urban landscape. Together we have investigated many villages and cities all over the world [points to the wall, where preparatory layouts for his publication *100 Lessons*

are fixed: photographs, plans, and sketches of settlements in Africa, Europe, and Asia]. Here, we were concerned about village structures, trying to explain the characteristics of each settlement as objectively as possible. We need a large vocabulary to express the significant qualities of each single place. We tried to establish categories and collect "good words" in order to be able to make new architecture from them.

C.K. and J.R.N.: In the works of the Hara School Architects we can discern a general theoretical approach. Can you explain what this approach is and how it relates to other theories?

H.H.: What we want to do is explain the things we see objectively. For example, if we tried to explain the design of an African village only using images of the buildings or our own impressions, it wouldn't be enough. We need more theoretical support and logical explanations, and then we stand a chance of finding the roots and the origins of settlements more easily. For this reason we have to establish a system

Hara House,
Tokyo, 1974.
Interior space created
by an inversion.

of language, and in doing so, we develop a sense that we are in fact working in a shared system of language. For instance, we use the Theory of Fields as it appears in mathematics and the physical sciences. In relation to those subjects, the definition of "field" is already well established. But we have to think about the meaning of "field" in architectural terms; we need to find parameters for describing *architectural* fields. The Académie des Beaux-Arts did not know the term "field"; they simply didn't have such a word. Nowadays, on the contrary, we often hear of "field influences", so we have to think about the determinants around a field. This vocabulary indicates a similar way of thinking among certain architects.

C.K. and J.R.N.: In terms of physical science, a field can be controlled by outside parameters which can be determined. The shape and qualities depend on the rules that constitute the field itself. In your Montreal City competition entry, you simply provided a number of urban elements and a set of rules.

H.H.: What I'm talking about is a semiotic field or domain, while the vocabulary of the Beaux-Arts consisted merely of "window", "roof", and "column shapes". This isn't enough, but somehow such attitudes still prevail today. In order to discuss matters of construction and design, the Beaux-Arts architects used plans, but we want to talk about domain, that

is, what happens in spaces of larger fields, how is it used? We don't ask, what does it look like? In the phenomenology of Edmund Husserl and Martin Heidegger, they referred to the experiences of people in space, while trying to refrain from objective words or definitions. However, we can try to express a certain part of such an experience. We might not be able to formulate our perceptions exactly, but I guess we can grasp some objective parts of a space and our experience in it, and so we use analogous words that were established in the fields of mathematics and physics.

New Architecture-Speak

C.K. and J.R.N.: In trying to discover what is communicable in architecture, you seem to be saying it has to be translated back into architectural geometry. Is that the meaning of the term "social geometry" which you often use?

H.H.: Yes. Maurice Merleau-Ponty described our spatial experience as one that is not translatable into language. I believe he is right, since by way of example, the experience of light falling on a wall is not possible to express in words.... [Hara draws a row of lighting schemes inside a dome]. Only in physical terms can we describe areas of darkness, bright zones and contrasts; we can also tell brighter domains from shaded ones. Of course, we have limitations in expression for our experiences; nevertheless we are trying to describe them in objective words. Just using the words "windows", "roofs" or "columns" can hardly express architecture—we don't use these terms any longer, but many have stuck to this old language. I don't know if we can succeed by employing these words, but at least I have tried to create another language.

C.K. and J.R.N.: It is interesting, however, that you have reached a demarcation line, beyond which it was not possible to go using analysis alone. In your studies of settlements you admitted that there were parts that you couldn't analyze....

H.H.: There is a limit to talking using just one vocabulary, but I have tried to broaden the field of possible expressions through these new words.

C.K. and J.R.N.: Husserl's phenomenology demanded that we go "back to the things themselves". In this respect your collection of architectural materials may culminate in a collection of "real" architecture—factual objects rather than abstract concepts. How do you transform the knowledge of village patterns and settlement structures into your real architecture designs?

H.H.: This is a really difficult theme. The one concept we often discuss, is how to create a topology. This is a very important point because topology can supply the connection between theoretical concerns and the solid world, between existing things and the conceptual level. Now it's getting difficult—I have to draw. Let's define a field as a closed domain. Every point within it can be characterized by functions, for example Phi [the name of Hara's office taken from Erwin Schroedinger's wave equation]—all of them have a certain value of brightness. In fact, this means topology of light. There are possibilities as well for topologies of sound, activity, temperature, moisture, and wind velocity. You can find many more examples if you want. We can describe them as mathematical functions. This is how we recognize the topology of space and we are always talking in such terms. It becomes so important, since specific topologies can really explain the characteristics of a domain. In the old days we used

descriptions like these [Hara draws a roof, columns, a basement, and a temple]. This might be what we now call "the old style of talking about architecture". Nowadays we have to talk in a different manner.

Diagrammatic Space

C.K. and J.R.N.: On the subject of architectural topology, can we talk about it in such a scientific, formalized way? What part does intention and fantasy play in this?

H.H.: I don't really understand the question. [Laughing] And I cannot talk about fantasy! If you want to create the space of a light field, by an opening in a roof—a skylight [draws a top-lit space]—we can determine this opening by reference to the lit space we want to create. But I cannot tell you if the opening is dramatic, beautiful, or in any way aesthetic! There are so many choices we can select from to produce a certain topology of light! You can draw roof-forms and openings *a, b, c, d* [draws more plans] which produce a similar lighting effect and are similarly shaped, but using these plans won't help you determine which is the most beautiful space or which is a bad choice. The only things we can explain are the diagrams themselves! We use this kind of topological theory[1] although we cannot make out if *a, b, c,* or *d* is the most aesthetically pleasing, but the theory is the bridge which enables us to talk together and discuss our thoughts on a similar level. We too are preoccupied by style: if I have to make a concrete wall space with a certain type of roof on it, the main concept in our thinking is still "space". The stylistic approach and the spatial approaches are completely different. I am always changing the conception of space; we're not wedded to any particular styles.

C.K. and J.R.N.: Here behind us are photographs of your new Kyoto Station. It is quite enormous, almost a city in fact! Architecture, when understood as a "field of conditions" comes close to urban planning, even when dealing specifically with buildings.

H.H.: Yes, you are right. Even if we are designing a small house, it has something of a city plan inherent in it. It is city-like in that sense.

Kyoto Station. Above: station plaza; right: interior canyon; below: roof structure and "skywalk" bridges.

Scale-less Scale

C.K. and J.R.N.: In your GA work monograph you don't make a distinction between different scales: you use similar techniques for all scales and mix them strangely at times.

H.H.: Of course there are peculiar characteristics of scale. Though many people tend to misunderstand it, I have always been interested in the 500 m × 500 × 500 m cube. Now we are attempting the next step. This is a cube of 720 mm, of which we have made five. We then enlarge that basic model a few times, while the differences between the scales are kept constant. The smallest model is 4.8 m³. We always investigate working on a huge scale with these kinds of box. After this process we will produce a kind of small box in reality, as real architecture. Using these cubes, we can think about problems that are the same on every scale, despite the specific problems implied by size; a 500m × 500m × 500 m cube has its own characteristic space. But there are still

enough similarities and topological principles in common. If I make holes to illuminate the inside, the same light phenomena will appear regardless of scale. In terms of fields, they might be totally equal or at least similar with respect to acoustics and air. I am very interested in this aspect of architecture. If we regarded style as the most important feature of architecture, we'd be talking about either such things as columns or the construction of the box. But if there is an elevator shaft in the big box there might be an analogous shaft in the smaller one, not necessarily a real elevator.

C.K. and J.R.N.: Would you use a term such as "inhuman scale"?

H.H.: That is the other side of the coin. Until now, we have been talking about space. Next we have to describe scale in a similar, adequate way. However, scale has too many features [sketching]. If you are working with a certain scale, various specific phenomena appear: one of them is "field", another one is "boundary"; then there is "meaning" and this is the

(mm)³ Projects, conceptual presentation of a series of 5 cubic houses, 1998.

(5,200 mm)³, (6,400 mm)³ etc., Ito House, Nagasaki.

most difficult characteristic in architecture. It is impossible to say everything in architecture, but it is possible to express a certain part of it. We cannot regard these schemes M and N together for example; it might be possible in a mathematical operation, but

difficult, no doubt. If we were able to find one feature for each of the phenomena, we still couldn't claim to have reached the limits of our descriptions of spaces in mathematical or physical terms. It's experience that can describe them all together, and here we can include the experience of beauty as well. In my opinion pure mathematics or pure sciences do not exist. Just because I'm familiar with them, it doesn't mean I can design good architecture. What I want to emphasize is that the knowledge of such characteristics could create a new distinctive architecture, rather than the architectural discourse of the style. With just this conviction I believe it's possible to create other kinds of architecture.

Outer Spaces

C.K. and J.R.N.: The Low Earth Orbit (LEO) designs are currently on show in the Shin Umeda Sky building. What are your thoughts on "cosmic architecture"?

H.H.: I was interested in extraterrestrial architecture, because the limitations are much more severe there. On the moon, for example, the difference between the light and dark sides is three hundred degrees centigrade. That minimizes the space available to a great extent. To give another example, I have visited many villages in the desert, which although not the same as the moon, allow us an approximation of the situation in general. It's appropriate to use the word "effective" to understand this architecture. The desert's inhabitants think in those terms themselves, so this makes them capable of creating good settlements. However the problems that such desert people face are serious.

C.K. and J.R.N.: The cosmos and the desert are extreme environments that you explore through your architecture. Do you feel imprisoned within the traditional field allotted to architectural intervention?

H.H.: From my perspective, there isn't a decisive difference between the "desert-scape" and the universe—both mean the same to me. We really ought to think about architecture in various environments. To put these constellations into words, we can systematize them by descriptions like "field", which we have already properly defined. The word "dimension" still poses a very difficult question. Though various scales are implied in the measurement of dimensions, it is still possible to have a common understanding of them. On the most simplistic level, people are aware when a small thing starts getting bigger. I haven't yet understood all the factors relating to dimension and scale. I am trying to develop ways of describing the various aspects of our experience, imagining particular environments in order to clarify the many. We can develop spaces without being concerned about size. Even if their scales or environments vary, we can still talk about them at the same time and compare them. By contrast with our Beaux-Arts predecessors, we understand this subject differently. When we were thinking about our recent design for the library of Miyagi City, we dealt with conditions of temperature, the acoustics, climate and so on, and therein lies the difference.

A New Humanism

C.K. and J.R.N.: Are these technological parameters sufficient to describe new conditions or social environments?

H.H.: I am well aware that technological or mathematical thinking cannot solve such problems, but they are at least of some help. In the same way that

E. T. A. (Extra Terrestrial Architecture) Project

the words "courage" or "meaning" are difficult to explain well, our rationale won't be enough to express how we continue to live, or how our environments change. In this regard, nothing is solved within science itself and it is no use thinking only in scientific terms. The kind of things that have to be taken into account today include taking stock of the growth in population; in Germany for example, the population is currently around eighty million, while the increase in world population is upwards of ninety million a year. The tasks for contemporary architecture arise from that kind of consideration. How can we get to grips with the reality of this information? Technology can't help here at all, but at least it is important in formulating the information. When I designed Kyoto station for example, I had to consider landscape, tradition, and history, but at the same time I referred strongly to the problems of the increasing population and population movement. It means, in fact, that all our methods are increasingly changing. Soon, even when we create a house for

Umeda Sky Building, Osaka, 1993.

five people, we'll have to keep in mind the ninety million people increase. We should bear this in mind when we think about contemporary architecture.

C.K. and J.R.N.: Kengo Kuma introduced a concept that sounds very interesting in relation to your work: "the designer of consciousness".

H.H.: Consciousness...function...modernity. What will our future environment be like? In India for example, many people are homeless and sleep on the streets. Every year there is this huge increase in the number of homeless people throughout the world. Modernist architecture as well as contemporary architecture doesn't recognize this fact; their terms of reference are mainly aesthetic. They work without an awareness of population figures; such a viewpoint for modern or contemporary architecture is nonsense. I can't stress enough the importance of considering this situation. Now when we discuss humanism we are thinking about a new humanism! Of course in the 1920s and 1930s, architecture was also taking human beings into account. Le Corbusier and Mies van der Rohe certainly did so. At that time, the world population was about one third of today's. The image of city and community fitted perfectly to that time and to its social programs. But what shall we do now in our contemporary architecture? Look

Miyagi Prefectural Library, 1998.
Above: general view; below: entrance lobby.

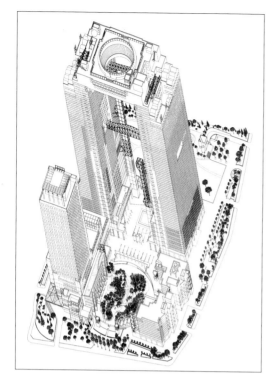

Shin Umeda Sky Building, 1993. Above left: site conception; above right: linked double tower and "Mid-Air City" platform.

here [draws a Mies van der Rohe skyscraper] Mies designed this in 1920, but it was only realized in 1980! It is interesting that young architects are thinking about things called "louvers" or are producing colored boxes—this is the new international or universal architecture. In fact it is the beginning of the new "Environmental Box" which is something that really fascinates young architects today. This "New Miesean Box" is an intuitive preoccupation and less theoretical. In this vein I am thinking of the young Swiss architects and Japan's Kazuyo Sejima.

Architecture for Ninety Million

C.K. and J.R.N.: You are currently selecting the photographs for a publication on Kyoto Station. Are you satisfied with the results of this project?

H.H.: [Laughing] I am never satisfied with any of my work! The recent Miyagi Library design is completely different from Kyoto station in every possible way. When the construction is finished, I am going to try to make a comparison between both projects. Simply put, the new Kyoto station is in a way sub-culture—culture for everyone! Popular architecture... [laughing] "Pop-Arch"! Miyagi is different; it is as it were high-culture. We used a completely different approach in design; Miyagi is "quiet" architecture, silent. In Miyagi, there will perhaps be five hundred people passing through each day. Kyoto station by contrast is pretty noisy, and some three hundred thousand people will rush through every day. It is very important to consider who we design architecture for. I would like to make architecture for ninety million people!

Note

1 Topology, a sub-division of mathematics, deals with the relationship between formations of points in space without regard to the scale and size of the formation.

Toyo Ito

August 13, 1997

*We met Toyo Ito on the uppermost floor of Ito's confer-
ence building. On a board prizes, medals, and awards
for Ito's architectural works were displayed. Functional
furniture and cool lighting filled an otherwise empty
room.*

The Tokyo Configuration

Christopher Knabe and Joerg Rainer Noennig: Is "Tokyo" now
an inescapable fate for everybody working in the
field of architecture in Japan?

Toyo Ito: I think of Tokyo as a whole image in itself
but having said that, it is an image that is incomplete,
it simply isn't possible to address the complete image
of Tokyo. Historically, Tokyo's architecture had a
predefined form and program that could be followed
and accomplished, but now the scene is very much
transformed. I think that Tokyo as a city is further
advanced than the individual pieces of architecture
which comprise it and that it is in a perpetual state of
revision.

C.K. and J.R.N.: Should the architects' task now be
to sense this advancement in change and development and to interpret that into architecture?

T.I.: That's not necessary but you do have to realize that a house or a building is not an individual or
isolated structure in itself, it is just one part of a
place in a city. Each element in this city exists as part

of a network that communicates with each other,
and each structure and network is relative to a more
general phenomenon.

C.K. and J.R.N.: Many buildings in Tokyo are strik-
ingly different in reality when you compare them to
representations in books and magazines. Do you
think that this is purely a matter of context?

T.I.: Here the problem is that during the planning
stage we try to connect the building to its surroundings and not to conceive of it as an individual entity.
When I come to look at a finished building I still have
the feeling that it is isolated and not related enough
to its environment, and that's a real problem.
The complication is that of the relationship between architecture and cityscape which developed
from architectural history. In the planning stage of
a house design you always try to fit it into the
surroundings and set up a relationship to its context.
Once you have started the construction however,
it slips out of that relationship and establishes a

T Building in
Nakameguro,
Tokyo, 1991.
Below: Tokyo
cityscape.

way of isolating itself and this is simply difficult to
avoid.

C.K. and J.R.N.: Previously, city planning was expected to shape the cityscape but this doesn't seem to
apply to modern-day Tokyo. You once described this
diminished architectural influence as "architecture
swimming in the flow of the city." Is the relationship
of building to architecture now an inverse one?

T.I.: In Japan until the 1970s the situation was
fairly static, architects felt a sense of responsibility
towards dividing cities into housing areas and business areas. There were decided points of view relating to the building and its context within the city.
Now it transpires that business architecture, for
example, has no context within the whole, only that
of its immediate vicinity. Architects now realize that
whilst some structures do form relationships, others
remain in isolation, so the perception of urban landscape is quite altered.

City Nomads

C.K. and J.R.N.: You have developed the concept of the
"city nomad", identifying the condition of the
modern individual moving through parts of the
metropolis without any real stability. Initially this

was a conceptual idea: did you anticipate it becoming a reality?

T.I.: I established this concept of the city nomad
about ten years ago, the time when Japanese

Yatsushiro Municipal
Museum, Kumamoto
Art Polis project, 1991.

Left: pedestrian perspective;
below: interior facade view;
bottom: cross-section.

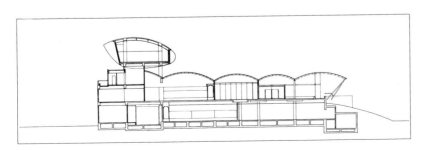

consumer culture was at its climax and when people's mobility was also at its height. These modern nomads are probably fewer in number now. Things aren't very different today, but the way in which mankind communicates alters as each new context is formed. As time goes by, the increasing problem is definitely one of space. Consider a person's house which forms a center from where all communication or information is transmitted; it is something absolute. Being a nomad doesn't necessarily mean that the living space disappears or shifts, but it does means that everything works in a decentralized way and in a mutual relationship. If we replace the words "dwelling" and "personality" with "human" and "dwelling" and apply this to the example of children, who used to go to a school which was close to their homes, but nowadays attend schools far away and have to travel long distances, thus dividing their time between home, travel, and school and not merely home and school, we can see that perhaps "home" now mixes with many other concepts and relationships. The movement between these is the reason I adopted the term "nomad".

C.K. and J.R.N.: So architecture no longer refers to fixed points as much as to networks of movement?

T.I.: I mean something slightly different: if you consider an absolute center the final object, then other lines that have no final point are merely transitional points. These transitional points should not be reduced to one type of architecture as the same principles can be applied to both housing and public buildings. Whilst public buildings are not so distinct from each other, they show the same tendency in development, as are all points of transition. Let's now look at the change in house functions. Take a house where a family used to live and imagine a smaller house in a different place where they might take holidays. The second smaller house had a specific function that was less than that of the main home. Nowadays the relationship between two such houses is split half and half, as the functions of each are more evenly divided. I recently had a project from a couple who live in Tokyo to build a holiday home outside the city. If you asked them which they consider to be their "real" home they would actually say the one outside Tokyo!

C.K. and J.R.N.: Martin Heidegger claimed that being and dwelling coincide. Do you think that a lifestyle that involves moving around so much creates an indifference to places to live in and to the city?

T.I.: I now believe that neither that assertion nor my nomadic style of living can hold one hundred percent true. We are left with this dualism then, and my architecture is now concerned with working between these two extremes.

Physical Self, Virtual Self

T.I.: The desire to stay in one place and rest and the desire to move to somewhere else are both inherent in a person. There is the actual body which is subject to gravity and that needs to eat and drink and so on, and the mind of the self which seeks virtual spaces. These are two different and opposing worlds, and are similar to the problems we have found in the question of where to live. The task of the architect is to accommodate both these points which might contradict one another and yet exist within each single body. One concept has to fit this situation—there needs to be one architectural answer for this dualism. Buildings now exist in systems of complex relations to one another, and this requires that architecture is not only physically lightweight but also mentally lightweight, which is "mentally light architecture." This architecture must be open in the sense that it can easily be rethought.

C.K. and J.R.N.: Perhaps the modern day convenience stores are an example of this mentally light architecture: people use them and move on. Do you see architecture becoming something that is itself consumed?

T.I.: Architecture is already the perfect object of consumption today! Nowadays it is easy to view housing and architecture in general as objects of consumption and this is the point where the problem of dualism occurs most obviously. It is now impossible to own architecture in terms other than conceptual ones; of course some people will choose to disagree with this.

C.K. and J.R.N.: Has architecture now lost its ties and relation to history, both past and future? Is it now only relevant to its present?

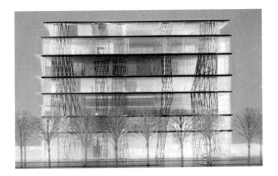

Mediathèque, Sendai, to be completed in 1999.
Above: main elevation; below: detail of facade.

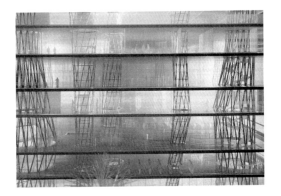

T.I.: In my architecture I really only look at the present. I want to look neither back nor into the future and the problem of "how shall I live today?" is the same problem as "what shall I build today?" The problems of architecture therefore exist on the same level as the problems of ordinary people. Maybe there was a time when people were building for ideals that belong to the past, or they tried to build their vision of the future, but not me. Coincidentally I think that the best way to think about the future lies in mastering the "now"—in that sense I must be an optimist! I think that I if I had grown up in Europe I would certainly feel differently about this. I think that Western people are led to a greater degree by their desires and aspirations about the future. I guess that architecture has always been very conservative. Filling the gap between the conservatism of the past and the needs of today is a task in itself, especially in terms of public buildings that are organized by very old-fashioned minds in Japan.

C.K. and J.R.N.: If you think about filling this gap, does this relate to your theme of "mental space, mental architecture" and is this gap one that lies between mental and physical space?

T.I.: I don't draw a distinction between the mind and physical aspects. What I recognize are two areas that must be bridged. The first of these revolves around the way in which mankind feels about its surroundings: we now spend more time with visual media looking at our computer screens and this virtual reality actually affects our real space and creates a real void to be filled. This is an increasingly large void. The second one is that which exists between the social program and the program of the architect himself. Let's take a look at a library to illustrate this, the public may have a program of their own for the library, but I think that a library has to contain more programs and operate as part of a network, so there can be a gap between the public approach and my own.

C.K. and J.R.N.: Let's talk about your work that was featured in the Visions of Japan exhibition held at London's Victoria and Albert Museum in 1991. Your installation was famous for its dark space with video screens lining the walls and floor, demonstrating what was then a newly emerging reality, a hyper-reality of virtual neon spaces that have now long been part of the appearance of central Tokyo's Shinjuku and Akihabara at night. A second room contained the installation by Osamu Ishiyama, in which many everyday products and even rather banal things were gathered, such as Coca-Cola vending machines, plastic monsters, Chinese lanterns, and so on.

T.I.: Ishiyama's exhibit represented a version of Tokyo in the daytime, while mine was that of nighttime. Shifting the view from day to night moves the city to its more virtual appearance. What I tried to do was to realize this vision of the night as something architecturally real in iron, steel, and concrete, thus transforming virtual space, which is a constant nowadays, into something physical.

Expression of Society

C.K. and J.R.N.: Can your involvement with virtual space be traced back to your relationship with

the architect Kazuo Shinohara who used the term
"abstract space" in a particular way?

T.I.: Back in the early 1970s when I first started
work as an architect, I was very attracted by
Shinohara's idea of abstract space. But I was soon
very unsatisfied with the self-contained and self-
referential nature of this abstract space, which was
too complete in itself and lacking in communication.
It was from this point that I wanted to develop my
own perception of abstract space. Virtual considerations did not exist then in the way that they do today,
so I now concentrate on the virtual aspects and the
importance of their role.

C.K. and J.R.N.: Can your perception of abstract
space be understood as a full integration of both
body and mind, into architecture?

T.I.: Postmodernism has long referred to the combining of various meanings and components: my
position is that it must be possible to express the
situation of society by combining different aspects of
reality. For me the position of each element, whether
it lies inside or outside the scheme I have developed,
is very important. Shinohara is, by contrast, less concerned with individual elements and their position

and more with a general image of society from which he derives a model for a self-contained simulation. Ishiyama's work also differs from mine in this sense: he combines aspects of everyday life, whereas as I use electronic and virtual media to express my ideas on society.

Integrated Circuit

C.K. and J.R.N.: Your design for the Jussieu Library in Paris resembles the programming of a computer chip. In your model you layered various programs into one space.

T.I.: That's right, and I am really interested in this layering of computer chips as well as the functional processing which makes up an integrated circuit. This layering is what I wanted to apply to the library, especially superimposing the two main components: that of people gathering and that of people reading books. I think that places where people gather nowadays are no longer limited to vast spaces such as European-style meeting places, city or town squares. Now there is usually a medium that promotes people gathering or an event that provides a reason for gathering, such as a sports event. In thinking of the library as a gathering place the medium was "reading books" so I endeavored to integrate one with the other.

C.K. and J.R.N.: Modern production methods and high technology attempt to minimize structural means, creating borderlines and layers of material in order to concentrate as much activity as possible in a small space. Could this be a metaphor for your architecture of screens, filters, and light structures?

T.I.: Yes, it can be looked at in that way. The architecture is light in the physical sense, and its borderlines are made as thin as possible, which also builds in the feature that it is penetrable. These physical borderlines have the potential to allow other layers through, and it was important to me that this effect was included.

C.K. and J.R.N.: Previously high efficiency and cost effectiveness were met by mass production and pre-fabrication. Efficiency can now also include a concentration of means, are you now including these considerations in your work?

T.I.: Optimizing the cost of materials may well come into it, except that technical methods are actually more costly than other traditional methods. If you try to make the borderlines thin you have to use very precise machines, and as these are expensive it doesn't necessarily follow that this type of architecture is economically effective.

C.K. and J.R.N.: These permeable borderlines seem to have various functions including that of screens that can simultaneously display multiple images, whether these are video films or slide projections. You have even used a type of net to display projected images; these nets have a neutral quality that allows the attention to focus on the pictures themselves. Would you say that your architecture is more concerned with image than with meaning?

T.I.: Yes that's exactly what I want to express. Architecture can function in a similar way to an installation, inasmuch as it can give priority to a display more than attempting to explain anything about itself. The projection on the exterior can itself have an effect on the building and can overtake any other meaning the building might have. The building itself is therefore never foregrounded in this type of work.

C.K. and J.R.N.: How does this affect your choice of material?

T.I.: When we decide on a material I don't think of it in literal terms: glass or wood doesn't have to work or be used as it is normally, but rather I consider what it is possible to achieve with and through this material. If the work is going to require glass I consider all the properties of glass, how it reflects, what variations are there in its appearance, and how many expressions can it have. If you think of a wooden table, that it is made of wood is less important than what can be "expressed" by the material. This way of thinking is fundamental to me, not only in making decisions about material but also as an approach for the architectural design. Often at this point in my discussion, I'm accused of wanting to do everything with monitors or screens! But naturally I realize that the physical body is still there to be considered. This aspect has to be given some thought but what the physical body likes and needs is pretty much the same as it's always been. What is clear is that there is no longer a need to accommodate only the physical body—the body and mind

Nagaoke Lyric Hall, Niigata Prefecture, 1996.
Above: interior view; below: plan of ground floor.

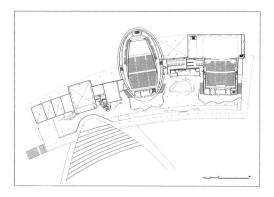

dualism is now inescapable and neither can be left out.

C.K. and J.R.N.: Going back to the Jussieu Library, you conceptualized place by means of parameters

of high information density and seemed to avoid geometry as such. This work however doesn't appear to have transported the intensity that you intended. You said: "I want to create places instead of form, a place that may have ambiguous boundaries."

T.I.: Yes, but I don't intend to create problems with geometry. I'm attempting to escape from self-referential forms such as circles and squares. It's a matter of choice and I prefer to work with flowing spaces rather than with strictly geometric ones.

Layered History

C.K. and J.R.N.: In escaping established geometry, do you think that your architectural experiences of a virtual Tokyo can be well communicated or applied outside Tokyo, or even outside Japan?

T.I.: Maybe it isn't possible to apply that knowledge directly to other cities such as Los Angeles, New York, or Rotterdam. I think that Tokyo consists of three layers. The first one goes back to the times when Tokyo was still named Edo [Edo became Tokyo in 1868]: the city structures that were built during the Edo era [1601–1867] followed natural conditions and formed a kind of urban spiral. The second layer was introduced throughout the Meiji era [1867–1912] and in the hundred years following the Meiji Restoration [1868–1968], when more geometric city patterns were imprinted on the first one. The third layer is that which has appeared most recently, in the last twenty years in fact, and this is the "information" layer. These three layers are imposed one on top of the other. What I like to do is to rework more of the first layer of natural structures and flows, digging it up so to speak. If it is possible to use that kind of idea and rework these initial concepts then that might well be worth analyzing and seeing if it could be applied elsewhere.

Hiroshi Naito

August 15, 1997

Hiroshi Naito's unique contribution to his interview lay in his use of drawings. Continuously sketching throughout, his explanations were thus made graphic, and covered details of his own projects as well as historical, architectural themes.

A Waseda Education

Christopher Knabe and Joerg Rainer Noennig: You graduated from Tokyo's Waseda University, a university which has a distinctive character and which fosters a self-confident and liberal spirit. Looking at your recent buildings and comparing them with the style of self-expression encouraged at Waseda, there seems to be a big gap. What has happened in between?

Hiroshi Naito: [Laughing] To me? That's difficult to say. From 1965 to 1972, there were student riots. I entered the university in 1970, but all the university sites were closed and the professors had escaped when the students became violent. The professors had no intention of talking to the students. When I began to study architecture there was quite simply no one to teach me. I read books, I discussed topics like society, ecology, and architecture, everything really, with my friends! At the same time, I was working in architecture offices, making models and drawings for competitions. The first and second year passed like that. After the third year I had to

complete a kind of design thesis. Usually the teachers expected some conservative project like a theater or museum but I wanted to challenge this. My project addressed the idea of chaos—everything was organic. Let me show you this project... [Naito takes out a folder containing his student projects]. I'm afraid it's not very good. It was twenty-five years ago [laughs]. Don't look at it!

C.K. and J.R.N.: Isn't this the thesis project that won you the Togo Murano prize?

H.N.: Yes, indeed it is; it is what I call "soft" expressionism. Following that, in my fourth year, I met Professor Yoshizaka. He was a pupil of Le Corbusier and worked at Le Corbusier's office in Paris from 1962 to 1963. Professor Yoshizaka made a deep impression on me. He didn't teach design in a literal or special sense, he taught more through general conversation. I talked to him about this project here, which contains some kind of flowing water, housing, and a cemetery. First I wanted to try to include any form of architecture in my one design, be it housing, garbage plant, a museum, or a theater. I talked with him about living and about life's complexities. I explained my concept to him—he listened at first and finally he uttered just one sentence: "You have to think about death, then your project will become very clear." That was his kind of teaching, he didn't discuss details.

Time and Temporality

C.K. and J.R.N.: How did the sense of temporality that Professor Yoshizaka mentioned manifest itself in your building design?

H.N.: This is a long way from these conceptual projects. When I set up my office in 1980 there wasn't much discussion of life and death. For the first five years we didn't have many projects and therefore could only afford to pay staff the minimum. Then I worked as a consultant in city planning. The Ministry of Construction had this huge regional development project, a concept covering an area of 200 km². We had to devise ideas for this area that would last fifty years. At first it seemed to be impossible. [Naito sketches a landscape.] This is the Yamagata district in the north of Japan in a scale of 1/2000, a city of 300,000 inhabitants. Here we have a railroad, a river, and *suiden* [rice fields]. This is a small city with shrines and temples. Working on this concept reminded me of Kyoto [sketches a plan of Kyoto city]. Kyoto is basically a square, laid out like a big gate to the mountains. All the temples are spread independently, positioned along the foot of the mountains, at the edge of the city...do you know why?

C.K. and J.R.N.: To prevent evil spirits or demons coming down from the mountains?

H.N.: Not necessarily evil ones. Basically this is where the dead live. Behind the temples lie the graveyards; they are a kind of sacred place. The temples function as a kind of spiritual guardian, an urban spiritual threshold or frontier. They are silent areas in contrast to the commercial city where many people live and move. The European scheme is quite different—city centers often have a cathedral with a plaza for example, and a surrounding wall. In the European scheme the center is the locus of maximum

speed, a point of gravity and is the "best" place. The plan for Kyoto looks quite different: it is a structure made up of the life of the community and the relationship between life and death. Every bureaucracy wants their system to be centralized: this means that in terms of city restoration, new commercial or cultural centers appear and the civic authority is right in the center. Keeping the example of Kyoto in mind while setting up the project for Yamagata, we had to find a concept which included public facilities and which would retain its validity for a long time. We have decentered the facilities and spread them around like the temples of Kyoto, surrounding the city. So the work we realized on the level of city or area planning started from Mr. Yoshizaka's idea.

Time was also a key issue in conceiving this structure. In architecture I suppose we have two main types: one is where time passes slowly—cemeteries, museums, and spiritual places. One of my works, the Sea-Folk Museum belongs in this category since time seems to flow very slowly there. The other type is commercial buildings—fast, accelerated architecture. [Sketches a fishing boat.] For people using this type of boat, life may be very short as the fishing industry can be dangerous work. If the structure of the boat fails or an accident occurs, the life span of the boat is shortened to only twenty or thirty years. Stored in the museum however, the boat's longevity is greatly increased, possibly by as much as two hundred years. In architecture too I think we have to deal with similar aspects. When I designed this museum, I had to think about very long time-spans, up to two hundred years. But in contrast, when I design a commercial building I need to retain a sense of the rapid changes that will happen there each year. The mistake of our architecture today is that we are confusing these two views. We have to look at the temporal dimension of architecture and should make a clear distinction between these two perceptions of time.

Fernand Higueras in Spain

C.K. and J.R.N.: Before you started working on your own here in Japan, you spent two years in Spain at the office of Fernand Higueras. He has been acknowledged as a major Postmodernist, having made those

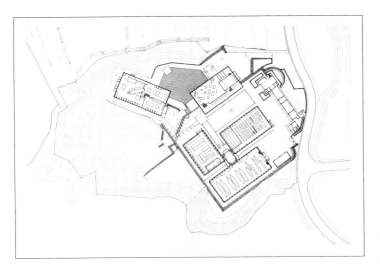

Sea-Folk Museum, 1992.
Left: site-plan;
below and bottom: exhibition halls.

pre-cast concrete forms—quite an anachronistic style. Back in Japan, what influences did you bring from Spain and what have you left behind in Europe?

H.N.: This is not easy to explain. After graduation I was working on the Master's course at the Yoshizaka Laboratory. At that time the Japanese architectural magazine *Shinkenchiku* [*New Architecture*], asked me to write a monthly column on Japanese architecture. I was twenty-four years old at this time, too young... [laughs]. At the same time Arata Isozaki was completing many of his projects month after month: big projects like the Fukuoka bank, the Kitakyushu Museum, and a library. I was young and rebellious, I wanted to challenge his opinions, polarize, and protest.

C.K. and J.R.N.: Is this the Waseda spirit?

H.N.: [Pausing] Maybe! For a year I wrote the column every month. After that I looked for an architect I could work for abroad. Unfortunately Louis Kahn had recently passed away and Alvar Aalto was dying. In the preceding years, Fernand's projects had been published in *a & u*, and *Forma Nuova*, and they made a big impression on me. Mr. Isozaki wanted to pursue a kind of philosophical approach to architecture, putting meaning into it and working with that meaning, a completely different approach from Higueras. So I wrote to Higueras saying that I would like to study in his office, he said "OK" so I went to Madrid. When I arrived, Fernando was in a poor way. In my opinion he is a kind of genius: he had succeeded at a very young age even though it took him eight years to graduate from the University of Madrid. When he was only twenty-three, he won the Spanish First Prize for watercolor painting. He was studying architecture, but at the same time he was drawing and painting. He won the prize the year after that as well! Later he wanted to master the guitar, so he studied and succeeded in this too. His guitar teacher was Andrés Segovia, the famous guitarist, for whom he later designed a house. After that he graduated from university as an architect. He immediately won first prize in the competition for Madrid's new Opera House, although its construction was finally cancelled. His was a real success story as an architect even at a young age. In the 1970s Spain was ruled and controlled by Franco's fascist regime. Fernando didn't like Franco, but at this time architectural journalism, and in particular

this magazine *Forma Nuova*, supported him. In 1978, when I went to Madrid, a kind of revolution had taken place: Franco had died and the journalistic conditions had changed. The left-wing parties elected the new President of Spain. All the magazines had changed their mind somehow, and Fernando became a victim of old age. He produced some projects but these weren't published. By the time I arrived in Madrid he was deeply disappointed and didn't want to work. I stayed at his office for two years, but it wasn't really a creative time for me so I decided to come back to Japan.

C.K. and J.R.N.: Other famous Spanish architects like Antonio Gaudi or even Santiago Calatrava are also structurally and aesthetically quite exceptional. Did the Spanish experience leave any impressions or images with you that might be found in your work now?

H.N.: When I set up my office I was always thinking about structural aspects and had discussed these with some structural designers and engineers fifteen years before. We hit on two main types of structural logic: the first is found in Gaudi, where every part is compressed [draws vaults and arches]; the second was probably created in Germany or England [draws a trabeated frame]. The first is the expression of Latin people such as Toroja, Gaudi, Pier Luigi Nervi and Calatrava, but normally we just use the second, more simplified, logical type. It is extremely abstract although convenient for calculating in situations such as an earthquake zone, since it is easy to solve. It is very analytical, and this is the reason people are astonished when they see Gaudi's structures. He put his buildings together in a completely different way: he used those "inverse rope and sandbag" models because it was extremely difficult to calculate. This is the analogical method, which is not abstract but rather organic. In Japan everybody has forgotten this method and I want to combine both. Such concerns had been important elements in Fernando's work as well as in the work of Gaudi.

Finding Oneself

C.K. and J.R.N.: In the brochure on the Sea-Folk Museum it seems that your attitude towards architecture changed completely during this work.

H.N.: When I began the work at the office I still didn't know how to create architecture. I couldn't find my way, so I set myself the task of trying to understand my work between the ages of thirty and forty. I tried out many different types of architecture and building [laughs]. Before the Sea-Folk Museum my design was, frankly speaking, not so good. Don't look at it!

C.K. and J.R.N.: It can't have been easy not belonging to a particular school, and having to create your own was surely even more difficult. We often classify architects by the school they belong to or their teachers: Kazuo Shinohara, Arata Isozaki, Hiroshi Hara, etc.

H.N.: These schools, as you say, usually form certain groups. However Mr. Yoshizaka always said you have to find your own way; this said, my early designs are nothing to be proud of. I can't show you [laughs]. Maybe later.... I did not belong to a group but I worked in the architectural office of Kiyonori Kikutake, where there were many famous architects at this time including Toyo Ito, Itsuko Hasegawa, and Tadasu Ohe. But they diverged and their methods became quite different in the end, although Toyo Ito and Itsuko Hasegawa were quite similar as Shinohara influenced them both.

C.K. and J.R.N.: So you belong more to the generation of Ito and Hasegawa than to the Sejima generation, even if the first two are a little older than you?

H.N.: I don't belong to any generation, I don't think this is so important, except for those who need to classify people.

C.K. and J.R.N.: Toyo Ito spoke about the ephemeral city and virtual space. Both of you regard architecture as something that has stopped being a product of the architect's self-expression or will; how do you feel about expressing your own attitudes through buildings?

H.N.: I don't want to express myself. When you have to create a building, you have to make so many decisions and you have to choose the best ones. You have choices between *a* and *b* which might be on the same level. The architect has to make difficult choices in an instant sometimes: that choice is down to me, and how I choose is *me*! As far as the architects in my office are concerned, I'm not prescriptive about wanting this or that kind of form, this taste, this design, or whatever.

Architecture for a Day or a Thousand Years

C.K. and J.R.N.: You described the design of the Sea-Folk Museum as being as rational and economical as possible.

H.N.: [Laughing] Because it had to be a cheap building! I really want to speak in Japanese to explain this as the problem is very delicate.... Since we are living in a capitalist society, the flow or cycle of money decides everything in the first instance. Architecture is quite important in that flow: it is the flow of capital that creates architecture. If you relate an architectural project to investments and to the people that are all somehow involved in that undertaking, you must see that the project can't be to do with you alone. Every project has its own pattern of capital flow. Government projects allow the money to flow from top to bottom like a tree, and even company projects disperse money in a similar manner. That flow of capital is only valid for the duration of the construction process. After construction is finished, other people start to use the house or building and form a new relationship with it in its final form. From that position there is a completely new flow in motion in the architecture and this is connected to program and organization. As time passes people will change the use of the architecture, and the character of the building will alter each time. If the architecture functions well, it should work like that. Take the Sea-Folk Museum for example: when I started the design project, the works to be exhibited numbered 7,500; after finishing the design there were 20,000. When the first of these buildings was actually completed we had to accommodate 30,000 exhibition pieces. At present, now that all the buildings are finished, the number stands at some 45,000! This is symbolic really, because when a building is "living" the program and use can be changed. In the normal scheme of things a building is designed and a fixed program for its use decided upon. When long spans of time are involved, the programs inevitably change. The building should accompany this change in program as well as in a real way. The time span from the start of design until the end of construction is really just a short chapter in the building's existence. It is usual that the client or owner makes or implies many specific requests and wishes, but this

Shima Art Museum, Toba Mie Prefecture, 1993. Above left: exterior view; above right: detail of roof structure; below: interior of main hall.

C.K. and J.R.N.: So this is different from the Miesean "open space", which was also supposed to be capable of varying functions and uses; the Miesean space did not have the option of aging, it had always to be new.

H.N.: That is very important. From the beginning the Modern movement was inherently insufficient in its tenets. The "Five Points of a New Architecture" by way of example, as Le Corbusier listed them—free facade, long window, etc.—never implied a statement about time. I looked for that specifically, but I found nothing. I think the Modern movement and its materials like steel and concrete had many more possibilities. So many architects do as they like, as the recent or Postmodern movement has shown, and this is because there is no dimension of time that architects could be aware of. If you have to make architecture just for one day for a hundred people, maybe there are some hundred possibilities. If, on the other hand, you have to build a structure that could last a thousand years, like the pyramids, there would be just one solution!

The Basics of Architectural Work

C.K. and J.R.N.: Talking of long time spans we are reminded of your writings about the "protoform". It seems as if you are referring there to a kind of archetype, an ultimate form that is beyond fashion and temporality. Is it the idea of "shelter"? You

influence has an effect on the architecture only so long as the client–architect relationship exists. The building has to last much longer than this initial client–architect relationship and therefore it should adapt to and follow the passing of time. In the future there will be other clients who reconstitute the building. Right now the architectural plans are here in front me, but we have to imagine the future of the structure as well, the future users, and the aging of the building.

described the Sea-Folk Museum with the phrase "sheltering earth"....

H.N.: You have to have a roof to keep out the rain, and you need a wall as protection from the wind. We have to do the simple things at first, not decoration such as artificial clouds on a roof. These things only have a short time-value (within that context they are OK of course). Short life-span buildings have their place, but so too do the buildings that are "built to last". What architecture can do in terms of virtual space is almost limitless since you can do anything on the computer. It's very interesting, you can have a lot of fun on your computer screen, but only architecture can make things that really exist, the real things. You should think about time when you want to create lasting architecture.

C.K. and J.R.N.: In your correspondence with Vittorio Lampugnani you both mentioned the term "architectural quality". In Lampugnani's definition this is "the exact translation of the needs and aspirations of an epoch into artistic form". Do you feel you express your work artistically?

H.N.: I have slightly different ideas about the quality of architecture. There might be two ways to express ideas and thoughts in the world nowadays, but architecture doesn't belong to the arena of virtual expressions. Virtual space has many possibilities and suggests many illusions, but the size or the height is still limited by scale. If human beings were five meters tall, then architecture could be quite different. We design using a scale that refers to our human size — 1.70 m or thereabouts. The human scale, which is completely different from the scale of the computer world and its created images, decides everything in architecture.

Photogenic

C.K. and J.R.N.: You have written that the significance of architecture is its "becoming," that is when it is completed. How does this "beginning" stage relate to the life of the architecture after this point of completion?

H.N.: When a building is completed the architecture seems to be most concentrated in that "moment". That is because of the architectural media, the newspapers, and the photographs that are usually produced at this moment. Everybody wants to become famous, and that's the time to take photographs. If they look nice, it's pretty good for the architect — the photographs are invaluable, and they become the best means of communication!

C.K. and J.R.N.: Working with protoforms, you strip the architecture of its excesses and it reaches a state of dignity. Is the idea of protoform a kind of counter-concept to that of the "consumption of architecture"?

H.N.: In Japan the economy has suffered many failures, maybe the highest in the world. I would like to clarify and correct this in relation to architecture. It is better to think long-term and to consider how things age instead of putting value solely on what the architecture is on completion.

C.K. and J.R.N.: You have included numerous technical drawings in *Kenchiku Bunka* [*Architectural Culture*]. Is there a direct link between basic principles of construction and the ability of a building to age and obtain a lasting value?

H.N.: Creating through images alone helps for works of short duration; engineering principles can change only over a long time-span, if ever. Concrete, steel, or wood doesn't change so quickly.

Low-cost Nostalgia

C.K. and J.R.N.: The Sea-Folk Museum exhibition room has tar-painted wood cladding outside which is between the first floor where there is a glass wall, and on the top where there is a glass top light. It seems as if a band of nostalgia is suspended between the two areas of modern construction.

H.N.: That's interesting....

C.K. and J.R.N.: And this band of nostalgia is able to connect the building to different times. Do you draw a connection between the materials and how they're treated and the idea of nostalgia?

H.N.: It is low-cost architecture. By using the old traditional materials we could reduce the costs of construction, so we did. If new materials had been cheaper, we would have used those. The owner of the building wanted it to last a long time. What I want to say is this: if we want to make a building that will last for a hundred years, we have to have a look at buildings that were built a hundred years ago. If you want to create a lasting building you have to study the old structures and their structural systems; this is the most valid point of reference.

C.K. and J.R.N.: Perhaps even the way they're put together becomes meaningful.... It is very impressive to find buildings that evoke such emotional intensity and are so impressive, when they were thought out so rationally and were strictly limited by budget and means of construction.

H.N.: I think that's right. Within such a tight budget, the materials for the structural system can only be like that. Even if you did the same project again, the building might not be different...it was so rigid! The budget was only a third of the average in Tokyo, so you see the choices were extremely limited. Initially I didn't like the *kawara*, the traditional Japanese roof tiles. In my student years I took no delight in those nostalgic, traditional materials or methods—I preferred pure expression. At first the roof of the Sea-Folk Museum was stainless steel, but what with the salt in the sea breezes, this would only have lasted five years, so we had to look for a more resistant material. The only other choices were lead tiles or titan steel. So we finally chose the *kawara*, which seemed to be the most adequate means of coping with the salt in the atmosphere. Having disliked them previously I changed my mind because of the material's properties. It became clear why the older forms of architecture had used them. Even the degree of the roof slope is just right for this kind of material—it is almost dependent upon it. I didn't want to create a traditional building but since I studied the traditional materials and construction systems the building developed in the way it has. The size of one tile is the weight that a carpenter can move by hand, and the tile joints were created through a building tradition that is three hundred years old. You simply cannot change or improve on this!

C.K. and J.R.N.: This kind of structure and this kind of logical approach to a building is like a narrative: it becomes a narration of the process, especially in the context of nostalgia. Atsushi Kitagawara—while his architecture is completely different—said that economics is a new kind of literature and that it too contains a narrative that can be understood.

H.N.: Tradition is not the image of reference. If you think in that way you're coming close to

Postmodernism. If you see tradition as technology you can see the other side. Making the tradition the image, which people like to do, so that it is really accessible, is a very dangerous route to take.

C.K. and J.R.N.: If the building has to express a very strong image, this image should be one of sincerity.

H.N.: That's right.

The Wind and the Earth

C.K. and J.R.N.: With regard to your current architecture, you designed the Dr. Makino Memorial Museum and it seems that you escaped from an archetypal style or a protoform. It could be said that it is "meandering".

H.N.: Here I started a new way of thinking and designing. I think that the building should be inserted in its environment—that is very important. The Makino Memorial is on a mountaintop and was designed following just one principle of utmost importance: how to create a relationship between a building and the earth. What was dangerous about the protoform was that once I had made it, the protoform could have been placed anywhere. For example, when the villages in Europe changed as places, the protoforms changed too. When I want to improve architecture, I have to think about the landscape or the earth itself. The Sea-Folk Museum seems so good and so perfect, but there are some critical points: the site was somewhat protected and quite flat. The Makino project differs from this, as it was built on an ungraded site and makes use of a "soft" roof. You might call it landscape work. I am not sure if the building will be all right, but I have tried to create the building in a way that responds to the earth. From this point on, wind force became a central element in my architecture. Normally we are talking about gravity but that is the same all over the Earth. In relation to the Modern movement, gravity enforced a similar structural system all over the world to create the International Style. We conducted experiments using models, and we found out how different the wind loads were, depending on their points of attack on the building. We found that wind had a greater effect on architecture than gravity ever did. If you start discussing wind loads

Dr. Makino Memorial Museum, 1998. Under construction.

you are very far removed from the International Style's thoughts on the nature of the cube for example. Discoveries about different elements have led to thinking about a completely new architecture. Consideration of elements like the air, wind, earth, and electricity can influence architecture in many different ways. The environmental conditions vary greatly in places such as Bangkok or along the Equator, but there you can find glass-fronted skyscrapers, which are greatly affected by atmospheric conditions. This is quite senseless—we have to change something. Even by taking the wind into consideration, the style of architecture changes.

C.K. and J.R.N.: Is your response to issues of the environment an attempt to find some secure place to start architecture anew?

H.N.: We were thinking about Miesean space, which implied gravity in one sense, but now I want to start thinking about the other elements or forces on the Earth. I want to look at the questions surrounding the creation of architecture in particular or special places. A lot of time is spent thinking about the structural system of the protoform we'd used in the past, but from now on we want to combine all the influences to generate a protoform. We want to include the values that can be derived from the earth and the landscape.

C.K. and J.R.N.: In making a protoform for one particular place, do you hope to leave the realm of "universal protoforms"?

H.N.: Over the last few years I have traveled around Asian countries and this is where I gained this experience and knowledge. The image of the universal space of modern architecture might have been the spaceship landing on Earth, but the question of how to connect a building to the earth is crucial; it depends completely on that particular place. It is now necessary to consider how the architecture can grow out of its earth.

Arata Isozaki

August 23, 1997

Our interview took place the day after Arata Isozaki had returned from a trip abroad, and his preoccupations were thus still focussed on the international architectural scene. Speaking with eyes half-closed, Isozaki was able to concentrate on the theoretical impulses behind his work, and produced some fascinating insights.

An Architectural Condition—
The ANY Conferences

Christopher Knabe and Joerg Rainer Noennig: "Tokyo, as a condition for Japanese Architecture" is a subject we have been discussing throughout all the interviews. The works of almost all the other architects we've spoken to, show some reaction to this city. In your architecture however, we found a different approach. You call it "anti-urban architecture." [Isozaki was born and raised on the southern island of Kyushu and embarked on his first architectural projects there.] Your work seems to have drawn great benefits from being created outside Tokyo.

Arata Isozaki: Yes, but this raises a more political subject: the relationship between the city authorities, the working conditions for architects, and their intentions.

C.K. and J.R.N.: In this context let's discuss the ANY conferences.[1] Peter Eisenman declared that the ANY conferences wanted "to raise architecture from the

state of a parasite to that of host," making architecture an essential means of creating culture.

A.I.: Peter and I were the two founders of the ANY conference. The participants in each case were selected mainly from local architects. We have held this conference seven times already, but we have never had a delegation from Germany.

C.K. and J.R.N.: Do you think there isn't enough interest in this kind of conference among German architects?

A.I.: I doubt that the ANY Conference officials—Peter, Cesar Davidson, myself or other younger generation architects—have much information about Germany, and perhaps German people have no interest in this kind of thinking. I'm not that familiar with the situation.

C.K. and J.R.N.: Nevertheless you build in Germany.

A.I.: Yes, and so do Peter, Daniel Libeskind, Rem Koolhaas—everybody has some project there. We

Daimler Benz,
Potsdamer Platz, 1998.
Urban development
block, aerial view.

looked for some key people in Germany to organize this conference there, but we couldn't find anyone. The initial four or five conferences were no problem to organize. The first one, for example, was in the United States—Los Angeles (1991); the second one was organized by myself in Japan (1992); the third in Barcelona (1993) by Enrique Miralles, one of the ANY trustees, and Pierce Lombard organized the fourth in Montreal (1994). Since then conferences have been organized in Seoul (1995) and in Rotterdam this year (1997). Arranging the conference depends on finding sufficient funds to invite twenty architects, writers, and artists from all over the world for two or three days. Financing it depends on each case: in Europe, for instance, the costs are lower and transportation is cheaper. In any case, we have no plans to hold a conference in France, but there are many French people, not necessarily architects, but philosophers and artists, who are frequently invited. In most cases in France, activities among the architects are organized by the state. There are almost no private commissions. The interest is mainly a public one and this concentrated power is very strong. In Germany every city seems to have different ideas, is controlled in a very traditional way, and is subject to the city's individual institutional rights and laws. These variations obviously affect the architects themselves. Some of the freelance architects, such as Rem or Daniel or Bernard Tschumi, work internationally but face a lot of red tape particularly in Germany. I'm often in a similar position. Having said that, Daniel had better luck with his Jewish Museum in Berlin. This came at a time of crisis in Germany and there was a lot of pressure from the Jewish population. I think it was this degree of pressure that made it possible to realize the project. I appreciate the difficulties involved in realizing these projects, as my relationship to the Tokyo metropolitan government is similar. Architects who are mainly commissioned by the government, give in some way the right answer to your first question about Tokyo as an "architectural condition," since we are subject to a city's regulations and bound by its agendas.

On the German Mind

C.K. and J.R.N.: In Germany there are diverse opinions with regard to architecture as an institution. There is perhaps a lack of theoreticians among architects of your generation who could influence new trends [Arata Isozaki is in his late sixties]. In Europe recently there have been few influential architects such as

Peter Cook or Aldo Rossi, while in Germany there's no one to take the lead. Perhaps a new interest in architectural theory is only emerging now.

A.I.: Heinrich Klotz probably helped to confuse the German situation, in my view because he became famous all of a sudden. In the 1970s he tried to follow some modernist streams and suddenly he changed his mind and became a post-modernist. Following that he made another big move into media art, and for a long time he was the director of the Architecture Museum in Frankfurt. He had a strong impact and his attitude was very fashionable. At the same time, he'd picked up the worst elements of American architectural fashion and brought them to Germany. This turned out to have a great influence on the students. People in the city and the established professionals are very much against that sort of fashion. We, the established professionals, have a responsibility to build cities and architecture according to social programs. At that time it seemed the American architectural trends lacked something like Aldo Rossi's contextualization of the historical city, even though that's a very old-fashioned modernist's view of the city. For the students in Germany this meant there were only fashionable streams to follow. There was no substantial core to influence what architecture and the city was about. There were long theoretical talks, by architectural historians, by philosophers, and by theoreticians; each had interests, but none of them could influence the whole architectural scene.

C.K. and J.R.N.: Theoretical discourse in Germany is still rather weak. It seems as if it is stagnating, especially if we think about the so-called Berlin connection and those architects who are determining the style and look of the city—namely those architects who follow Germany's Hans Kollhoff and Paul Kleihues.

A.I.: In the middle of the 1970s Kleihues appeared as a kind of producer, organizing exhibitions involving about nine architects. I was one of them. He organized the International Bauausstellung (IBA) in Berlin and made a positive contribution both in Germany and abroad, not only in the theoretical sense but also in managing how architects are invited to construct parts of the city. Many international politicians made the trip to the Berlin IBA hoping to find something modern, and they were surprised to find something more classical and conservative. The design idea for reconstructing Berlin is very close to that of the nineteenth century and not the twenty-first.

C.K. and J.R.N.: It seems that this was a missed opportunity. The conditions were good, including financial and political support, making it an opportune time for the consideration of a more modern scheme. There was a lot of commitment too and many good architects were commissioned, but finally nothing new appeared.

A.I.: That's right—nothing new!

Against Stasis

C.K. and J.R.N.: Can it be said that one of your intentions, in your own work, is to try to escape again and again from fixed ideas?

A.I.: That's true because I don't want to become static. This is my concern as an architect and on a personal level. I don't want to maintain my status in society like great professors, academics, or as some heads of organizations do. I never wanted that kind of status. Other honorary professorships or doctorates, are not of interest to me either. Many people yearn for that kind of prize especially towards the end of their life but since I passed sixty I decided against accepting any. And those I have accepted, are only for buildings I have collaborated on. My feelings about material things, including prizes, relate to my experience of the war because that left me very confused. At eighteen I had lost all my family. At that time I had nothing and ever since I have wanted nothing in terms of property, possessions or prizes. In a city such as Tokyo many buildings are constructed as a product of people's desires. Capitalism however, is not people's real desire. Instead I think the city is composed of every kind of desire. Desire itself is the basic condition for life, indeed it is probably the purpose of living. This raises the question: what is the purpose of your life? What is the purpose of your being? I never know the answer, but it is something people have to consider and have to find an answer to. As regards this question, I don't want anything, I try to be a kind of "nothing", a kind of void is what I am always striving for.

Oita Medical Hall (1959–69, annex 1970–72), exterior view.

C.K. and J.R.N.: It seems that you favor rapid and continuous change in your life, which keeps you moving forwards, and stops you becoming "heavy" or stagnating. There is probably an artistic sensibility and intention in that.

A.I.: Or a psychological interest. What I produce as an architect is "heavy", neither light nor transparent. I think that city architecture itself has to be materialized in three-dimensional, solid heavy materials, such as concrete, or stone. It's not necessary to try to attempt anything "floating" or transparent. If I wanted to proceed in that way, it would be better to design on the Internet or using virtual media. Those kinds of media are always transparent and light and disappear easily. My life, however, in contrast to my architecture, must be kept "light".

C.K. and J.R.N.: How would you feel about an Isozaki School?

A.I.: If a kind of Isozaki School developed it wouldn't be what I wanted personally. The name belongs to me and I do not want to continue my profession through disciples or my children. I asked my children not to become architects, and not to think of following in my footsteps. A studio or a single architect's office is just for a single person's activities. It is completely unnecessary to ask family members to succeed you, although it is still common for many Japanese architects to try and educate their children in the same field.

Ruins and Evanescence

C.K. and J.R.N.: We have seen your drawings of the Tsukuba Center building as a ruin. Designing ruins seems to be very important thing to you. You seem concerned to describe things in a state of deterioration, not in a perfect state but in a way that rases questions about their existence later. For example: how long they can last and in what condition?

Tsukuba City Center, 1978–83. Detail of central plaza.

A.I.: I have learned both from Europeans and Orientals. I learned from the Orient that everything exists in a state of flux, even though city architecture and objects have their own life, all are born, will decay, and die. It is a process of change, decaying, growing and decaying again. Only changes are eternal. What happens is that some crisis will dictate the state of ruin but everything is to be reborn again. This "cycle-orientated" life is derived from Japanese thinking or Oriental thinking as a whole. Such an idea stands very much in antithesis to Western thought on architecture. To the European mind, architecture is eternal, and this

Hiroshima Electric Labyrinth. Isozaki used pictures of the devastated city to illustrate his essay "City Demolishing Industry."

sense of eternity is materialized through monuments. An attempt is made to keep these monuments alive and to support the regime the monument was designed to honor. Inevitably conflicts arise when the monuments outlive the regimes. This idea of creating eternity is the key to European architecture. If there is any concept of the term "eternity" it is defined differently in Japan. The Japanese concept is one that engages both life and death; everywhere there is construction and ruins. Perhaps both ideas are based on our different cultural perceptions of time.

Architecture and Change

C.K. and J.R.N.: How would you define these two perceptions?

A.I.: The Oriental perception of time is always contained inside the materialized being, while in Europe, material exists in a space-orientated framework, in an absence of time. Space and time in the European context are, as Immanuel Kant says, *a priori* for every being, and this applies to architecture and its, dare I say solid, fixed images. Space and time in Japan is not *a priori*, it belongs to every being. From the beginning of my theoretical work I have been concerned about how we should think about time in architecture. The great German philosopher

Martin Heidegger tried to define being itself in relation to time, but in Oriental thought, this isn't special or innovative since we already have this concept. Time, for us, is always inscribed within being. Architecture is not a fixing of images; in the design process we have to realize that architecture is always growing or decaying. Within the design we manipulate both growth and decay, and these can be interfaced inside virtual computer images. Despite the great benefits of using computers in design, there still comes a point where you have to stop and freeze the design in order to materialize it. I call that "computer and process planning". Materialization is the beginning of a new life, and if the lives of buildings move in the same direction that people's do, they will surely encounter change and eventually their end. The location of the building will dictate the change inflicted upon it—war, earthquake, or typhoons sometimes destroy buildings entirely. So you see, in that sense, eternity is impossible. If architecture is technique, and if designing architecture is simply the technique for creating monuments, then everybody in the West must have understood intuitively that there can be no definite object, which doesn't change. Herein lies a major contradiction. In some ways Western architects understood that buildings literally disappear, are damaged or ruined, but their intention was without exception to keep what they have built, what they thought was beautiful,

Oita Prefecture Library. Above: exterior view;

below right: plan of first floor;
below left: plan of third floor.

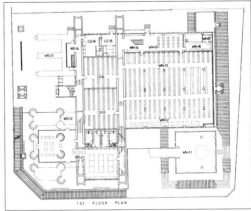

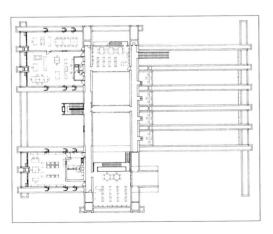

and what they intended to last a thousand or ten thousand years. In the Orient however, there is an easier attitude towards deterioration and destruction especially in Japan, and in particular in Tokyo. So these two cultures present the extremes: monument and anti-monument, or object and anti-object. In my own architecture I try to engage with this process of changing process as a method of organization.

City Demolishing Industry

C.K. and J.R.N.: Do you incorporate elements of both the European idea of revolution, which rejects what has gone before, and the Oriental idea of smooth and flowing development, as a "continuity of crisis" in your work?

A.I.: Yes, always! There are always some conflicts and these culminate in crisis. In 1969 I started as an architect and had no projects actually to build, only theoretical work. The first thing I did was to write a collection of essays entitled *City Demolishing Industry*. At the same time I wrote *Process Planning*, a kind of design theory wherein I organized the design of the Oita Prefecture Library. My intuition from the middle of the 1960s was that cities grow "invisibly". In such a way the material will be dematerialized, construction turns into deconstruction, and the structure is dismantled. Everything in every process undergoes change.

C.K. and J.R.N.: Do you set yourself the constraint of abandoning works after finishing them?

A.I.: This leads to yet another contradiction. Let's take Tokyo where I didn't have much work at the time. If I was to build in Tokyo and somebody was to say "the life of your building has finished and we want to destroy it," I would say "OK." But thirty-five years ago I designed the Public Library in Oita: over time this library became too small and the government asked me to design a new one, five times larger. The old library had finished its life. The city was going to knock it down but local people campaigned to keep the building. Ironically, in view of what we've just been saying, the city finally decided to keep it as a monument! Work on the new one was completed recently.

Crisis Equals Opportunity

A.I.: With the library in Oita, I was asked to renovate and restructure my own building, changing it from a library into an art gallery that would display my own work. So, as the building ended one life, it started a new one. I had some difficult problems to solve. The reason for keeping that building as a type of monument was the city's attachment to the exterior image it had had for thirty-five years. It was ironic for me that I couldn't change my own building in order to transform its function from a library to a gallery. I simply couldn't touch the outside. As it was built such a long time ago it doesn't conform to the new security earthquake design code, so I had to change the supporting structure. To do this we had to recalculate the entire building in another way. We could not interfere with the structure as a whole, but had to add some support hidden underneath or behind the old structure. There was no reason to keep the building. It could have been destroyed, but the city wanted to keep it, obviously it was not my place to decide. When a building is finished, the architects give their own work to the city, and to the society. After completion, I have to give the building up as it is the property of the city, and tackle the next project. Time always evokes very different and unexpected situations and I can never foreseen this.

C.K. and J.R.N.: You seem to have invented a working style which may be characterized as a creative machinery for dealing with the unexpected. It seems as if you installed this machinery to force your progress to continue almost automatically, with crisis forcing changes and change leading to new crises.

A.I.: Even if you planned your life perfectly, such a plan could only work for a maximum of ten years: if not before, then certainly after ten years, a crisis would emerge. Architects up to the age of thirty are considered to be in a learning period; between thirty and forty they can develop their own ideas and personality, strictly by their own design. After forty, however, society puts greater pressures on you, history generates pressures of its own, and family does too. Other influences will also force your method to change. By the age of fifty you may achieve more social status and this again forces change in another way. These crisis cycles are not wholly within our control.

Haishi Kaishi, "Mirage City", exhibition model.

Zeitgeist: Spirit of The Times

A.I.: I was in my thirties in the 1960s, after the occupation by America, and we had a big fight with American organizations because of their security treatment. A cultural revolution characterized the 1970s and I worked for the "Expo" in Osaka and for Kenzo Tange. In the 1980s I was very much involved with the design of the Tsukuba Science City Center Building, and at that time I had to reorganize my own design methods completely following a crisis. If you pursue one design method too rigidly, your method won't respond to the changes in society and you will be easily forgotten. In the first half of the twentieth century prophets such as Le Corbusier, Mies van der Rohe, and maybe Frank Lloyd Wright, were able to develop their own styles as a type of twentieth-century *Zeitgeist*—the spirit of their times. This lingered until the 1950s, when the younger generation stopped following their ideas, and recognized them only as the old masters. This generation began trying to find new directions, but they did not come up with many new ideas. This formed a crisis for the modernists in the 1960s as there wasn't any one mainstream in the world of architecture, but rather several small streams. The dominant *Zeitgeist* disappeared and no one felt the need to replace it.

In the second half of the twentieth century there are probably various *Zeitgeists* and a great deal of diversity.

Diversity—Kumamoto Art Polis

A.I.: I thought it might be possible to undertake a project like the Kumamoto Art Polis[2] in two or three places at the same time. In doing so, I wanted to challenge the bureaucratic way in which architects are commissioned, because this is the only way to change society. Coincidentally I tried to change the situation in general, where established corporate architectural offices get all the commissions from local governments. This condition has been a difficult one in Japan from the middle of the 1980s. The younger generation of architects has had no way of approaching these very closed bureaucracies. I agreed to open up the commissions and to introduce the younger generation of designers to competitions for public buildings. I have tried this for almost ten years now. For the Inter Communications Center (ICC) Gallery, Haishi Kaishi Project [the artificial island on the coast of Macao], twelve young architects were invited to design and develop my original ideas. Similarly, I have worked to promote women

Okayama West Police Station, 1997. Exterior view.

architects in organizing the Kitakata Public Housing Project. I also try to encourage new architects, run my office, write articles and books, and as paradoxical as it may seem, each of these activities represents the same thing to me. In Japan we've adopted the French word, *écriture*, and each of my activities is simply a different form of *écriture*. The methods involved differ for each activity whether designing *écriture* or writing *écriture*, but for me this isn't divergence but running in parallel.

Economic Bubble—Bubble Buildings

A.I.: In general, Tokyo is governed by a rather conservative set of conditions which in turn govern its building commissions. The number of interesting projects becomes fewer and fewer, and I can't find enough opportunities to introduce architects because of this decrease. It has been a difficult situation after the economic bubble burst, and public building commissions fell in number everywhere. Tokyo developed quite well economically at the end of the 1980s. But since then the economic situation in Japan has changed dramatically. At the beginning of 1990, some public commissions by private developers were stopped immediately, others continued only until

1995. Tax money that was active in the economy moved to the government's public sector. This allowed local government to build some public buildings over the last five years. Since 1997, however, there has been no tax revenue flowing to the local authorities, not even to the Tokyo municipal government. I have criticized the government in Tokyo because of its super, large-scale projects such as the City Hall, the Museum of Contemporary Art, the Tokyo Forum, and the Tokyo Edo Museum. Those buildings were developed selfishly, their concepts or the idea in the architects' design were the same as would apply to a building one tenth of the size. On such a huge scale I think they look like bubbles: this isn't the fault of the architects, but can be attributed to the desire for over-sized buildings. I guess it's the same with the new Kyoto Station by Hiroshi Hara. He, of course, has a different point of view as the financial conditions during the bubble economy allowed the government itself to be more liberal.

C.K. and J.R.N.: Did Japanese architecture forget to develop long-lasting concepts that would outlive the economic bubble?

A.I.: That generation were simply too busy to think or re-think concepts, or progress in their studies. There was no architectural discourse in Japan at this time and in reaction to this I started the ANY conferences in the middle of the 1980s. I think that now is quite a good occasion for new concepts as architects aren't as busy as they were during that period. It is somewhat paradoxical that I worked outside Japan when the work in Japan was increasing dramatically. During the time of economic growth, most projects were handled by private developers with whom I didn't enjoy working. My projects mainly consisted of public buildings. The Tokyo metropolitan authority forced the production of these large-scale buildings, and after the Tokyo City Hall Competition controversy, things became difficult and they never commissioned me again.

C.K. and J.R.N.: Was your competition entry too subversive? Did they feel attacked by it?

A.I.: Yes, and at the same time I criticized a lot of their attitudes.

Polarities—Architectural Politics

C.K. and J.R.N.: In one sense you have to, and want to, criticize through your architecture; but at the same time you depend, to a degree, on commissions from those you attack. Katsuhiro Ishii characterized you as a non-conformist guerrilla fighter.

A.I.: Yes, maybe! I don't believe in simple dichotomies: "this is good and this is bad". I think more about what lies between the polarities. Local governments compete with each other, in the same way as private companies, and if you are on bad terms with one side, you can still have good relations with the other. I think it is possible that criticism is not necessarily only good or bad.

C.K. and J.R.N.: Do you sometimes feel like a "blade runner" then? Always at the cutting edge?

A.I.: Blade runner? Yes, you have to do it that way. The contradiction is that conceptually architects are against capitalism, while professionally they are supported by it. Attacking capitalism also includes criticism of the architects' profession itself. In that sense it does not seem like criticism to the outside but is criticism of us, and of myself. This is necessary, as the social structure would remain static were it not for this complicated relationship of criticism.

C.K. and J.R.N.: Kisho Kurokawa understands himself as a social engineer, and Kengo Kuma states that architecture will be the sole profession that is capable of supervizing or ordering all the available technologies in life. The architect is assumed to be universal in outlook, mediating all the ambiguities in society. Do you see yourself as such a universal architect?

A.I.: I have no idea whether I am universal. Kurokawa and probably Kenzo Tange still believe in it, or they simply have good connections that allow them to appear so. At the same time, Kurokawa and Tange are competing with each other. Kengo Kuma is concerned about ideal appropriation being the most important duty of architects. This means finding the optimal means of solving spatial situations. This is understood as a way of using the media and is less concerned with traditional methods of gaining power. I try to stay apart from those social structures. In this position, probably a traditional one for artists or intellectuals, I try to maintain some distance from society in order to be able to criticize and in order to create culture.

Notes

1 Eleven inter-professional conferences held at varying locations from 1991 to 2001: Los Angeles 1991, Anyone; Yufuin, Japan 1992, Anywhere; Barcelona 1993, Anyway; Montreal 1994, Anyplace; Seoul 1995, Anywise; Buenos Aires 1996, Anybody; Rotterdam 1997, Anyhow. The next conferences will be entitled Anytime, Anymore, Anything.
2 A regional architecture development project on Kyushu Island in Southern Japan, not far from Oita, Isozaki's home town.

Tadao Ando

August 29, 1997

His powerful voice resonating throughout the office, Tadao Ando's presence was felt at the interview before he even arrived in the room. The discussion was enlivened by Ando's vivid curiosity, his scribbled diagrams, and his invitation to a passing client to join in the session.

Communicating Architecture

Christopher Knabe and Joerg Rainer Noennig: On your recommendation we visited the Church with the Light before this interview. The church is very impressive and having seen the building itself and felt its strong simplicity and clarity, it almost seems more difficult to talk about.

Tadao Ando: That's right! A building exists to be seen and to be experienced as you have done and not to be talked about. That is a message I would like to convey: there are so many people involved in architecture, whether they are designers, critics or even visitors and I think everyone has a different perception of architecture, a different attitude. I think people should try to experience buildings in body and spirit. These experiences can't be expressed with words.

C.K. and J.R.N.: In that case how can anyone communicate your architecture or its most important features?

T.A.: First of all, the language of architecture is the product itself—the building. Architecture speaks

through buildings and their spaces, but these spaces are difficult to express in words. There must be various places that you have experienced before you come to a certain building and these are what you might call a "prologue". We conceive of spaces in terms of how we are reminded of them—there are no words.

C.K. and J.R.N.: You said once that architecture is a kind of war, that one ought to fight instead of indulging in words. This seems to be a recollection of your boxing career, and perhaps it refers directly to the self, to fighting oneself rather than someone else.

T.A.: First of all, I don't mean to say that architecture is a sort of war. But the process of creation involves the process of thinking, and I was trying to say that such a process of thinking is a fight. To create an architectural act involves a kind of excitement too, in order to come up with ideas. But I think there are two aspects in architecture: there is

Church with the Light, 1989. Above left: interior; above right: ground plan; below: the architect's office appendix building, 1997. Interior axonometry.

an architectural vocabulary or language that could be conveyed through the buildings, but at the same time the personal experience of space would give a person a certain image that was communicated from the building itself. Therefore I think that verbal as well as non-verbal aspects are the two components which represent architecture.

Reality or Virtual

C.K. and J.R.N.: Talking about architectural representation, we'd now like to turn to your famous pencil drawings [there is a presentation scheme of the Kagoshima Urban Egg project hanging on the wall]. This is the kind of drawing everybody knows; they are very special. However representation in architecture, for you, seems to be about nature, the environment, climate, and culture. In your terms architecture represents a certain place and its special conditions and spirit. Speaking to architects like Kengo Kuma, and in other statements by young

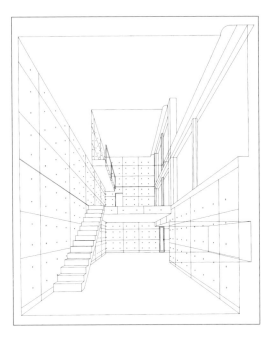

architects, it is clear that they are trying to make use of other media, like CAD and virtual reality, to

Sumiyoshi Residence, Osaka, 1977.

enlarge their vocabulary in architecture. In some cases, they claim these media have the same presence as built architecture or even more so, and that computer reality could represent a "reality of place."

T.A.: There might be those people who are satisfied that their designs can reach a certain level of perfection in the form of CAD or virtual reality. In my case, of course, we would use CAD as a tool, but ultimately we aim for creating architecture where people can actually experience the space and experience it as their own reality. Talking about virtual reality for example, if I wanted to buy a pen out of a catalogue in New York, of course I could do that, using all the communication tools available. In that way I would experience the space virtually, crossing it from here to New York, and therefore that is a spatial experience based on that virtual reality, but at the same time there is another spatial experience which is the reality. In today's world, it is even possible for some people to live within conditions of virtual reality. In any case you need to clearly identify your own place and where you are standing, where you place yourself within that environment. If an architect, for example, just wanted to create space

within the frame of virtual reality, he would need a completely different frame of reference from his conventional experience. He would need to work within the field of the imagination. In our case we are living in reality, with particular ways of seeing, deciding what sort of building is to be built at a specific location, seeing that building actually going up, and finally witnessing its completion and having people moving in and living there. That is our reality. Therefore I cannot imagine myself being confined to the realm of virtual reality since I am living in this reality today. It is possible, of course, assuming I could live on and work on in reality that I could also be constantly aware of that other virtual reality, and thus I could work in the best of both worlds! Did you hear about Dolly, the sheep that was cloned? We might ultimately have human clones, and then the question becomes is that reality or virtual reality? If we had human clones we would assume that this person would live just like any other person. Is that our reality?

C.K. and J.R.N.: Perhaps similar problems arise in today's architecture. We really should reconsider what happens to the actual world beside this new virtual one, what happens to the "old" physical

Chapel on Mount Rokko, Kobe, 1996.

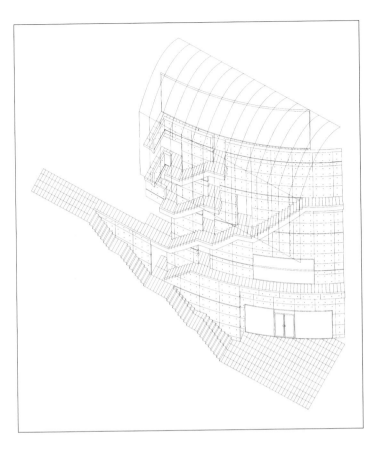

Gallery Akka, Osaka.
Axonometric drawing.

reality. In response to a film about you, your staff said that in relation to your work, you would "eat architecture"—virtual reality won't matter if someone needs to "live off architecture" in that sense.

T.A.: Eating architecture! Physically speaking, we can well do without virtual things. Mentally or spiritually though, we have all sorts of information around us today which is not necessarily fundamental to our eating or living, but which is a real need. If you look around, there is a lot of virtual information that we consume on a daily basis. Even in our everyday life the surrounding environment already incorporates all kinds of virtual aspects, so this becomes another "true" aspect of reality. To an extent virtual reality is already part of our lives, it's already within us.

C.K. and J.R.N.: Yes that's undeniable. We have to work with this realization, but on the other hand we probably need to maintain the non-virtual space of the tactile and of substance and emphasize its presence. Since the development of virtual reality, do you think that real space needs to be stressed more than ever?

T.A.: I don't think we need to emphasize real space that much.

C.K. and J.R.N.: Nevertheless, even in Europe it might be no accident that a number of architects have started to engage in a minimalist way towards more sensual spaces, with the intention of keeping some specific aspects of architecture as intrinsic—"the basic or original space". Peter Zumthor might be a good example.

T.A.: He came here about ten days ago. He really wanted to see me. He used to have a big beard, and when he went to visit the Church with the Light, he shaved it off! I guess entering that building was a serious matter for him.

C.K. and J.R.N.: What a triumph for architecture!

T.A.: I didn't join him on that occasion, so I don't know what his real impression was, but we did talk

Above: Kyoto Garden of Fine Arts, 1996;
below: Gallery Akka, Osaka.

about spatial experiences. You've visited the Church with the Light yourselves and experienced the space there, but the real part of that experience ends once you leave the building. I place great importance on creating architecture that continues to live on in your mind after you have left the building. The physical reality ends when you step outside of the architecture. After that it depends on whether you can keep that experience in your memory. And I think that this is not only valid for Japan: in the 1970s and 1980s there was huge economic development throughout the world. During that period, it was forgotten that architectural space, and spatial experience in general, live on in the human mind and are not just a momentary sensation.

Memory and Space

C.K. and J.R.N.: Architectural experience must depend on how people discover space. For example, when visiting your Gallery Akka, here in Osaka, we spent about an hour just exploring ways around the building. The excitement of finding a new corner, a new staircase, a tunnel, or another balcony left a big impression on the mind. There might be a relationship between the time spent in discovering a building and the intensity of the memory that remains.

T.A.: I think architecture exists for human beings not only for practical, physical needs, but also for their spiritual existence. It becomes a spiritual living space for human beings as much as anything else. That was forgotten during Japan's period of economic growth when colorful, exaggerated buildings appeared all through Japan. Of course I don't really know how people have access to my work. I just know what I feel about my work, and I conceive my buildings in their environment in a kind of psychological space, and not merely within the real physical space.

Prototypical - Kansai

C.K. and J.R.N.: We mentioned Peter Zumthor before and his appreciation of your work. In Europe your architecture is regarded as almost prototypical

Chapel on Mount Rokko, 1986. Left: interior view; below: axonometric drawing.

Japanese architecture. Nevertheless we sensed some opposition to your work here in Japan; might your architecture have a more problematic stance at home than abroad?

T.A.: I don't think that is true. I receive many commissions in Japan as well. I am accepted and I do business here in Japan, which was well reported in the English newspaper *The Guardian*. However, they did write that Ando lives outside the so-called architectural community, and that he is independent. In Japan, this architectural community is centered on Waseda University and Tokyo University and some other university architecture schools. The tendency is to exclude people who do not belong to them. That is the opinion among experts. Since you have talked with those "experts" already and asked for their opinions, you'll have found that they don't look favorably on me, as I'm not part of this architectural community.

C.K. and J.R.N.: It was exactly like that.

T.A.: If we want to speak about definitions outside Japan, I find that people abroad don't evaluate us as narrowly as they do within this island nation. We should be able to compete with each other through what we produce or what we design. As it stands today, the current architectural community is such that the people who design architecture are graduates from Waseda or Tokyo University, and the

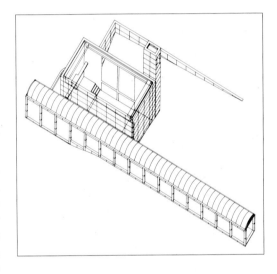

people who criticize architecture come from Waseda and Todai [Tokyo University] as well. So, given that situation, it is very difficult for me. At the same time I think it is very interesting to live so independently from them.

C.K. and J.R.N.: One fact that remained constant during the interviews was that the architectural community has apparently developed a strong network among its different sections. There are these schools, their pupils and teachers, and somehow they remain very close to each other for a long time, in their style and in their thinking as well.

Museum Fort Worth, Texas, 1997.
Below: site plan.

T.A.: I personally have no sentiments against that community, and I think it's fine for that community to exist, but I don't wish to belong to them. Even so it is stimulating for me in the sense that of course people inside this group tend to attack those outside, and therefore the latter always have to do their best to create architecture. When a German person, for example, looks at my architecture I think that person would look at the architect and the work of the architect. Their society wouldn't pay so much attention to the group to which the architect belonged, their background or the architect's community. I think my position has both good and bad points.

C.K. and J.R.N.: It also implies another aspect of Japan's architecture, its regional distinctions. There is a polarization between the Tokyo-Kanto area and the Kansai district [Kyoto, Osaka, and Kobe]. It seems that you have become a kind of local symbol for the Kansai area. How do you feel about being a Kansai hero?

T.A.: Well, the Kansai people try to compete with Tokyo, but Tokyo people don't think about Kansai people at all. [The inhabitants of Kansai are renowned for their comic talent; however people in Tokyo don't necessarily share the same sense of humor.] So I don't think it is a matter of competition between these two regions. I accept that Tokyo is the center of

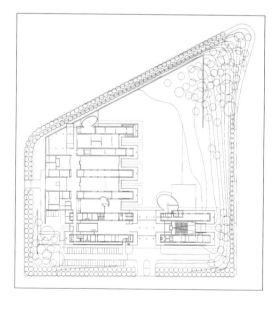

the cultural sphere and that's enough for Japan; but I do my work here in Osaka, Kansai. First of all you can see that the Japanese architectural community is rather closed, exclusive and Tokyo centered, and then there are the universities in Tokyo, Waseda, and Todai, which determine the architectural community of Japan. I am an outsider in all aspects![1] Working here in Osaka, I can comfortably pass on my thoughts to Tokyo or to the rest of the world, so it's a very convenient position. The Japanese architectural

Hyogo Prefectural Museum of Modern Art, 1996.
Above and left: models.

community is a rather difficult thing to work with—very difficult.

C.K. and J.R.N.: But it seems as if you have some fun with it too.

T.A.: I don't socialize with them very much. But when Norman Foster or Christian de Portzamparc come to Japan, they come to see me. Many overseas architects want to visit me quite often, but no Japanese do—they behave as if I don't exist!

Self-education and Motivation

C.K. and J.R.N.: Working in Osaka certainly provides you with the freedom and independence you need to continue the personal struggle you have mentioned. You traveled a lot in Europe, Scandinavia, and Russia, but from where did you develop your own style, and from where does your inspiration originate?

T.A.: There are various books you can get hold of about Greek, Roman, or Renaissance architecture,

but literature is not real experience, it is only "virtual". So in order to study architecture, it is best to go and study the real architecture. If you want to study the Acropolis, then visit it and read books about it—it's best to do both. That's how I taught myself. When I was interested in Renaissance architecture, I visited Florence and I learned a great deal from books written by Michelangelo.

C.K. and J.R.N.: Whatever your personal struggles, it seems that you have managed to turn this inside fight into a very calm final expression. Having successfully solved a number of building problems in such a way, what challenge can there be for you in the future, what keeps you running or shall we say, fighting, in architecture?

T.A.: I think the ultimate objective that I had in mind was to create a space where you are able to interact intensively with the human mind. Silence provides the best opportunity for that. Having visited various kinds of architecture throughout the world, I realize the diversity that exists and really think it's good that we have various types of architecture and architects. I am the type that pursues my own approach and there are others, and that is fine. Since human beings live in nature, I pursue an architecture where you are able to contemplate the relationship between human beings and nature seriously. The buildings are there to be occupied by humans and the kind of space that I'd like to create is a space that makes them happy by simply being there together.

C.K. and J.R.N.: The path you are following has a truly personal style, but this always runs the risk of becoming too rigid. Perhaps to avoid this, you have recently started to rework or rediscover traditional Japanese architecture for yourself, looking at its particular sophistication.

T.A.: In order to avoid becoming set in my ways, I always try to be conscious of what is going on around me, in society at large in terms of world events, as well as a few more personal influences. There might be people who become too rigid, but hopefully that's not me.

Twenty-first-century Architecture

C.K. and J.R.N.: What are your future projects?

T.A.: [Lifts down some models.] This is a project in Dallas, Fort Worth. It was a competition we won, and now we are in the process of designing it. There in the corner [points to the left edge of the model] is Louis Kahn's Kimbell Art Museum; it's pretty close. Here a glass box is used to cover up a concrete box, so the glass is outside the concrete. I believe the twentieth century has been the century of glass and concrete. I think these are materials representing extremes, one is transparent, and the other is simply massive. So I wanted to come up with a new type of architecture that would fit the twenty-first century, transparent and yet non-transparent architecture, non-transparent architecture that becomes transparent. You can see through all the greenery and the trees, and I wanted to come up with architecture where there is no clear border between the trees outside and the architecture. In essence this is just like the *engawa*, the veranda in Japanese traditional architecture. This traditional architecture is not the only influence for me; I've been influenced greatly by twentieth-century architecture and therefore wanted to create something more transparent. These glass and concrete boxes are used currently. We have a very three-dimensional space within the concrete box. [Moves over to another model on the ground.] This is the museum project that we plan for Hyogo prefecture to commemorate the reconstruction after the Great Hanshin Earthquake of 1995. These two museums are our way of trying to approach and express our idea of twentieth-century architecture. I always want to have new challenges. Sometimes I fail, sometimes I succeed.

C.K. and J.R.N.: This is a challenge that looks backwards while heading forwards.

T.A.: Yes, that's what I have in mind. I have no way of knowing whether I will be successful or not, but I hope it works. There are many young people who are willing to become architects, and as an established architect I think it's our duty and responsibility to stimulate those young people. When I feel that I am no longer able to stimulate young people with my work, then I must have reached the point when I should stop designing.

Note

1 In 1997, just after this interview, Tadao Ando accepted an ordinary professorship at Tokyo University.

Osamu Ishiyama

October 9 and 14, 1997

Osamu Ishiyama was so keen to pursue the issues raised in the initial interview that he suggested a second, follow-up date, where he was able to focus on a specific number of projects. The interviews were held within a week in Ishiyama's office at Waseda University, Tokyo.

Architect–Teacher

Christopher Knabe and Joerg Rainer Noennig: Immediately after graduating in 1968, you founded your design office "Dam Dam." Can you talk about that period?

Osamu Ishiyama: I didn't work for many other architects. The most influential teacher then was Yamasa Yoshizaka [1917–80] and his theme was to "continue by discontinuity." This then became the main theme of Dam Dam. It is a design method whereby no architect has a central role in dictating the direction of the work. Everyone wants to design, myself included, and all of the members participate in that process. Our task is then to see how we might achieve successful results through this approach. It is a combined effort but I don't mean that in the sense of collaboration which might imply a compositional approach. What Yoshizaka meant in "continue by discontinuity" is to continue to work on a design and then to let go and to discontinue designs, and continue with another perhaps, in an ongoing movement.

C.K. and J.R.N.: Can you explain how this affected your work at the time?

O.I.: All my work, past and present and that of the laboratory are designed that way—my Kannon-ji Temple design at Waseda [Tokyo] for example, made a year ago [1996]. This attitude doesn't mean anti-composition. The typical dialectic used by Buddhism is "say no to everything" and it is from this perspective that the designs are generated.

C.K. and J.R.N.: That attitude of rejection can also be found on your map of world architecture in your laboratory. It draws attention to three specific areas of modern architectural significance, the old European, the American schools, and Japan. You have titled the generation of Japanese you belong to "Stray Berserkers," which describes samurai warriors who lacked governing lords to order them.

O.I.: That is actually a historical phrase used by Fumihiko Maki. Maki belonged to the elite establishment, his family originated from the Takenaka

Kannon-ji Temple, Tokyo, 1996. View inside altar room.

construction corporation. Before my generation, all architects came from rich families or from families in which the father was chairman of a major company [Fumihiko Maki is in his sixties, Ishiyama in his fifties]. From my generation onwards architects came from more ordinary families. I think that from the point of view of this social change Maki called my generation "Stray Berserkers."

C.K. and J.R.N.: That a group of architects has been given such a name, indicates that architecture has perhaps stopped fulfilling some of the social duties that were formerly attached to the profession but are now gone. Is that really so?

O.I.: As a student I learned about Hans Hollein who said: "Everything is architecture." From that position architecture certainly appears very democratic.

C.K. and J.R.N.: Toyo Ito, Itsuko Hasegawa, and Riken Yamamoto are slightly younger again [all in their forties]. How would you characterize your role in relation to that generation?

O.I.: The nearest architect to me is Katsuhiro Ishii [in his fifties]. All the others are rather strange to

me. Their understanding of their profession is quite different from mine. Of course, I can't define myself, by myself!

C.K. and J.R.N.: You graduated from Waseda University's "Laboratory of Architectural History." What kind of impact has the Laboratory's historical approach had on you?

O.I.: We were never taught by historians as such and there weren't any historians involved in designing. But as I learnt historical methods I could place myself in relation to various historical aspects, in a wider historical context.

C.K. and J.R.N.: In your position now as a Professor of Architecture at Waseda, what kind of architecture are you trying to shape and what features are you keen to promote?

O.I.: This might not be a very straightforward answer to your question, but I am always very eager to present my work in magazines not under my own name but under the name of the university laboratory, "The Ishiyama Laboratory at Waseda University." That is quite a conscious act of mine. There is an architectural office of mine outside the university and my clients try to persuade me to make all of the presentations purely under my own name. But I think that it is very important to maintain the published work under the name of the laboratory and the university. In terms of educating future architects, I pursue the ideal that architectural education should take at least ten years and that's the idea I push forward at this university.

C.K. and J.R.N.: Does the university strive to be an "architectural factory"?

O.I.: There must not be a contradiction between my personal work and ideas and that of the "architectural factory".

C.K. and J.R.N.: Your background includes an historical approach. How does this sit with other architectural methods such as scientific research?

O.I.: Since I have learned history I know how to make my works relate to an historical context so that different aspects should be able to coexist. Educating students is not about teaching the facts of the architectural environment—rain, wind, and snow, and then mechanical and structural engineering. Basically we must teach them that there are clients and other people in general outside yourself that are of importance, and demonstrate ways of creating architecture alongside these relationships. I aim to deconstruct the notion of architecture and the architect. I don't think that "architect" is an ideal profession as it exists by implication in today's very establishment orientated society. It is really important to express these ideas to the students and for them to realize the variety of people that I encounter. Educating students in design methods is only a small part of their training—they should see the architect confronting clients, or witness the complaints that have to be dealt with, because coping with all the problems inherent in the industry is a far more important training.

C.K. and J.R.N.: Do you find the students and their enthusiasm stimulating?

O.I.: I am in no way influenced by the enthusiasm of the students. It is not that I am using the laboratory name in publishing just to elevate myself but to show that public architecture can be done by university professors, which is something rather uncommon in Japan. The Japanese system is quite rigid and you are not generally permitted to have two professions at the same time. Now Tadao Ando is starting to teach at Tokyo University, this means that officially he'll stop being the head of his design office.

Time Traveler

C.K. and J.R.N.: Your work seems to demonstrate your curiosity with extremes—a feeling for improvisation and for perfection at the same time, is that accurate?

O.I.: That's my intention. In a way I set myself the task of protecting Japanese craftsmanship.

C.K. and J.R.N.: Do you favor either an avant-garde or conservative approach at all or do you always combine them?

O.I.: I have always had my doubts about both the straightforward high-tech and the advocators of styles, so I don't limit myself to either.

C.K. and J.R.N.: One critic said, "Ishiyama is a time traveler," because of this talent for combining past and new technologies and with neither seeming to take precedence.

O.I.: What you say is right and as I was not trained in early Modernism such as that of the Bauhaus in Germany, I am free to combine the two methods.

C.K. and J.R.N.: Combining Japanese craftsmanship with everyday considerations might well produce a direction that isn't straightforward. Is that intentional?

O.I.: That's not really my intention. I don't want to disturb a straightforward way of thinking and design; my method is very natural and straightforward to me.

C.K. and J.R.N.: You took part in the Visions of Japan exhibition in London at the Victoria and Albert Museum [1991] along with Toyo Ito and Katsuhiro Ishii, each of you depicting a different perspective on Japan. Ito's room was futuristic, magical and somehow "unreal" whilst yours dealt strictly with reality. Is "reality" what you are predisposed towards?

O.I.: Firstly let me explain something about the exhibition in terms of how it was organized. Arata Isozaki arranged the exhibition and he was also its main curator—he wanted to express the cultural identity of Japan through the symbol of a game. The rooms were not necessarily representative of each architect's work. Isozaki chose the themes. As

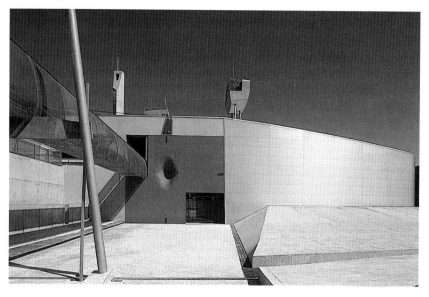

Rias Ark Museum of Art, Kesenuma, 1994.

Left: view east towards the entrance zone.
Below: elevated technical space.

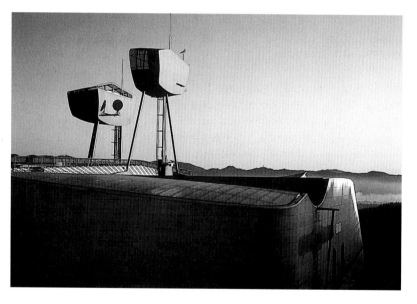

regards Toyo Ito and your question, I can't believe in the future in the same way that he does. I think of the future as something that is continually collapsing and that is the fundamental difference between Ito and me.

C.K. and J.R.N.: Nevertheless some of your work contains fictional elements, and you have created buildings such as the Light Coffin in Chiba prefecture—this is also known as Dracula's House. How do you explain the inclusion of this fictional element?

O.I.: In Japan non-fiction always transcends fiction especially today and therefore I remain most interested in reality. It is not that I complement my architecture with fiction since I view fiction and architecture as two separate media. In my work they are placed together but I keep th°eir differences in mind.

C.K. and J.R.N.: In relation to your Rias Ark Museum [Miyagi prefecture] you are quoted as saying: "The most boring things around today are art and design, and it seems that functional things have progressed several stages beyond them," and that "we must show how interesting the 'actual' truly is." Does this equate at all with your working style; does it point to your working with a more "hands on" design technique, unlike Ito who uses the computer almost exclusively to create architecture?

O.I.: It is a misunderstanding that I use my hands to produce my designs. If you look at Ito's work, the designs look as if there were totally computerized but my curves and the lines in the Rias Ark Museum and in the Kannon-ji Temple are produced mathematically and not by my hands. Bearing mathematics in mind you might say that my designs are actually more computerized than Ito's. Even the handrails and all the curves in my designs are produced mathematically and certainly not by hand. I don't use CAD for the drawings but other than that all the curves are computer generated.

Humor meets Architecture

C.K. and J.R.N.: In your essay "Small Accidents, Small Houses" [1995] you promoted and envisaged a "happier" type of architecture. Have you succeeded in finding or developing "architecture with humor"?

O.I.: I have not been able to produce what I aimed for in "humorous architecture". I am very aware of our position in the international architectural scene. I'm in the Far East and for me it is very important that I don't produce extremely serious architecture: "seriousness" is the field of European architects but I feel I can best compete with this by using humor. Europe has always been the center of history, the center of the world. There is an extreme distance between this center and my base in the Far East. When I was a student I had to learn all the European history of architecture because in my opinion the history of architecture just happens to be the history of European architecture. I studied Gothic, Roman, and Rococo architecture, but these are not really related to me or my feelings for architecture.

C.K. and J.R.N.: Are you therefore concerned to have notions such as "pleasure" and "laughter" given more credence in architecture?

O.I.: My aim in producing humorous architecture had its peak at the Karakuwa-Tairo Bata Gekijo

mid-summer festivals for which I produced designs [1988–91]. There we had the figure of an ox as one of the floats, and stating that this ox festival float was architecture, was my way of saying physically that I want to produce humorous architecture. Another example of this humorous style is from my work in the 1970s, my fantasy villa, Gen-an [1975].

C.K. and J.R.N.: What is your aim with this type of architecture apart from the fun aspect?

O.I.: You have to understand that I want to deconstruct "architecture" and "the architect"—these are my aims.

C.K. and J.R.N.: In what shape do you think criticism can usefully be applied to the architectural phenomena present in Japan right now; can humor also affect criticism?

O.I.: From my point of view I'd say that criticism is not applicable in any term that implies "seriousness", but only through a sense of humor. It might also be interesting to think of this in terms of European and Japanese differences.

C.K. and J.R.N.: In the 1980s you wrote *The Laughing House*. Was this an expression of your optimism?

O.I.: My vision might not truly be called optimistic, but my attitude and the way in which I work should at least bear an optimistic quality.

C.K. and J.R.N.: Let's talk a bit about optimism in relation to movements within Japan's general architectural scene and perhaps mention the Haishi Kaishi Project too.

O.I.: I was involved in designing the general theme of the Haishi Kaishi project [an artificial island on the coast of Macao]. I feel that the essential point about that project is a notion of borderlessness that doesn't recognize states, and whether it finally goes to Taiwan or to mainland China is of no concern. It is optimistic in the sense that it expresses a real idea of borderlessness.

C.K. and J.R.N.: Is it borderless only in a nationalistic sense, or also in terms of lacking vision?

O.I.: It is best not to have any direction now.

Kitsch Europeans

C.K. and J.R.N.: In the examples of Japanese design that appear in Europe it seems that there is an almost inherent need to draw attention to the distance between each place. At an installation directed by you and Arata Isozaki at the Venice Biennale Pavilion, a feature was made of the Kobe earthquake [this earthquake in 1995 claimed more than 5,000 lives]. Was this to emphasize distance?

O.I.: It was not an expression of rejection towards the Western world. There may be a way of saying that things exist differently and run parallel to one another, but it is not intended as a didactic statement.

C.K. and J.R.N.: You have encountered European architecture first hand: during the Nexus World Project [Fukuoka 1991] you worked side-by-side with the cream of Western architects including Steven Holl, Rem Koolhaas, Christian Portzamparc, and Mark Mack. What did you gain from that experience?

O.I.: Well I had a lot to experience with them there but I lost something too.

C.K. and J.R.N.: What kind do you feel you lost there and how?

O.I.: I remember walking with Rem Koolhaas in a traditional-style Japanese garden and Koolhaas stated that there isn't really that kind of structure in a Japanese garden. I contested that indeed there is such a structure, but this was extremely complex. When Koolhaas built the apartments in the Nexus World Project he copied the external wall of a Japanese castle and its base of stones with a completely kitsch approach. I protested against that and told Rem Koolhaas that when I have a chance to build in the Netherlands, I will copy the windmills in a similarly kitsch manner!

C.K. and J.R.N.: That might be considered to be European avant-garde, but has obviously provoked your disinterest in European ideas.

O.I.: I have always been disinterested in European architecture in comparison to other types of architecture. But then at the beginning I was likewise disinterested in Asian architecture. My feelings did not change suddenly after collaborating with European architects and in my thirties I have to say that my taste for European architecture was limited to the work of Antonio Gaudi. I was in my forties when I first saw Le Corbusier's Ronchamp and I thought it might be a public toilet.

Writing Architecture

C.K. and J.R.N.: As well as being a professor and architect you are also a prolific writer, at times working on half a dozen books at the same time. Which provides more interesting goals for you, the architectural projects or the writing?

O.I.: Both have the same value for me.

C.K. and J.R.N.: In what respects do you find the two fields are connected?

O.I.: There is no clear relation between writing and building architecture. They are different topics and the way in which they are important is peculiar to each.

C.K. and J.R.N.: Do you think that architecture lacks the ability to "fulfill" in some respect, and that literature can compensate or complete where architecture falls short?

Gen-an Fantasy Villa, 1975.
View towards the entrance.

Waseda Sajikiyu Public Bath,
Naruko, 1997.

O.I.: It is not that my writing completes anything lacking from my architecture. They still exist independently. I don't believe that architecture expresses any ideology or thinking that should be expressed in writing.

C.K. and J.R.N.: One of your books is entitled *Building a House with an Akihabara Feeling* [Akihabara is Tokyo's "electric town" famous for its huge electrical goods stores and huge video advertising screens]. What are the main arguments in this text?

O.I.: One of the most important things I wanted to say in that book is that anyone can build houses and my belief is that the importance of architects will decline in the future.

C.K. and J.R.N.: Ryoji Suzuki mentioned your interest in houses built by laymen. Does this type of architecture provide exciting territory for you to explore?

O.I.: I am also interested in Ryoji Suzuki's "barracks studies" [makeshift structures designed and built by people who are not usually involved in architecture]. What interests me about these barracks studies is the sense of freedom that I can find inside them. I want to say that architecture doesn't have to be so professionally determined and that it really isn't necessary to be an architect in order to build a house. In that sense I am also pursuing the study of barracks.

C.K. and J.R.N.: That brings into question the education of the professional architect. Riken Yamamoto complains that engineering is now emphasized at

the expense of creativity, do you feel that architects are becoming more management orientated and that creativity now lies in the domain of laymen?

O.I.: I don't think that Riken Yamamoto's point of view applies to Waseda University, where the education is centered around the expression of personality and the self in relation to artistic design. Engineering doesn't dominate at that university, but generally speaking architecture is classified within the field of engineering in Japan.

Buddhism

C.K. and J.R.N.: You once said: "To understand Japan properly one always has to recognize Buddhism in all places." Is this related to a reinvention of Japanese identity following the recent onslaught of Western influences?

O.I.: You might, for example, feel a sense of strangeness and mystique about Akihabara: that strangeness is, in reality, based on Buddhism despite the obvious modernity of that area. It is not the case that Buddhism has been dead for some years following the war—it has always been alive and has influenced Japan's cities.

C.K. and J.R.N.: Is this also how you would differentiate between Western and Eastern cities?

O.I.: The substantial difference between Japanese and European cities is in the lifespan of buildings and this is directly linked to Buddhism in Japan.

Here we don't think that cities have to last more than perhaps fifty years and we are happy that buildings change. To the European the belief is that cities might exist forever and that the buildings should have a strong structure. By contrast, Japanese cities don't rely on that type of invincible structure. In other words you might say that Christianity is systematically constructed, whereas Buddhism has a strong affinity with "nothingness."

C.K. and J.R.N.: In this vein what do think the rest of the world might learn from Japan?

O.I.: Japan will present the world with the idea of a city that is not "hardware" orientated.

C.K. and J.R.N.: Another one of your book titles is *We Build the Best Towns in the World*. Where is the best town, or where will you build it?

O.I.: I don't mean that "we build the best town", in that sense. The act of assisting in or recreating existing cities is of greater importance to me. I wasn't thinking of any particular location, I was thinking about cities we already have.

C.K. and J.R.N.: You mentioned getting away from the idea of "hardware". Can you explain further how Buddhism can coincide with technological considerations?

O.I.: All hardware technology that now exists is derived from Western technology, Western concepts, thought, and constructions and is totally unrelated to Buddhism. But I think that the evolution of media technology might now have some relation to the Japanese cultural background. The reason for this is that this new media is separated from reality. In contrast to ideas of space in relation to architecture, this "media space" only exists inside of the self. That notion is an extremely Asian one, hence the Buddhist reference.

Architect's Coffin

C.K. and J.R.N.: How do you foresee Japanese architectural thought directed and articulated in the future?

O.I.: Architecture has already disassembled itself, and the problems of the concealed and sheltered space are at an end. The "new space" must be expressed through media technology and space of any importance will be created within this framework.

C.K. and J.R.N.: This seems to be part of the general outlook of today's architect–designer? But Ryoji Suzuki said that space is getting lost and that "space is an almost dirty word to me," so he refrains from using it. What kind of architecture is architecture without space? Will it be reduced to skin and form which contain nothing of importance?

O.I.: Once again what we are discussing is this "Akihabara feeling" with houses built by laymen, people building their own houses, and this is the state of things that I'm concerned with. Over the next five or ten years when computer technology is further evolved, we will witness everybody having the ability to design their own architecture and houses by themselves.

C.K. and J.R.N.: And the architect disappears?

O.I.: Yes, he disappears.

C.K. and J.R.N.: Is this a "happy" disappearance?

O.I.: Happy, yes. The problem now is not how to make things but how to communicate them. Right now we are developing ten "ready-made" houses at the laboratory which we are going to sell. Our concept is to let the users design the houses. Specific points, which they can design, include the rooftop, the colors, and the designs of the doors. What we are working on now is not designing houses, but on how to facilitate the consumer in designing houses by themselves. We are also investigating how to encourage people to buy them at the end, and how to advertize and communicate this idea.

C.K. and J.R.N.: In a way this idea resembles your work with the Light Coffin which was basically a deformed shelter that was left for the inhabitants to create something from. But the question still remains as to whether you were representing the will of the architect in its distorted surface?

O.I.: That kind of deformation is possibly the only design left for me as an architect. The theme of Dracula's House, the Light Coffin, is the disassembled family. The clients for this project were two men, not the common definition of a family at all and that marks the true importance of the house.

C.K. and J.R.N.: It seems that you want to question your profession on many levels. Does that also include working for clients of diverse backgrounds with perhaps extreme or eccentric taste?

O.I.: I don't really think that the male couple in Dracula's House are eccentric. Sure, they don't conform to the traditional definition of family, but they are not that eccentric. I might well have had the intention of using their design request to free myself from conservatism—I think that is what was really happening, something inside myself.

C.K. and J.R.N.: We have touched on your interest in communicating architecture to a wider audience. How do you feel this can be realized?

O.I.: The language we use in architecture right now is only communicated by means known to the architectural elite. A lot of terminology doesn't really mean anything to people outside this group. How to establish an architectural means of communication with the population at large is an important topic right now.

Architectural Sabotage

C.K. and J.R.N.: Dracula's House is your 1990s architecture—it is like a tin barn. Can we draw a conceptual relationship from that with your first famous work, the Gen-an houses of the 1970s, which are basically tube-shaped villas assembled from industrial sheet metal?

O.I.: You are right in saying that both are connected conceptually, the common theme is geared towards "nothingness." What I should just add is that this "nothingness" doesn't necessarily mean nihilism.

C.K. and J.R.N.: In both cases the main feature of the architecture is the ordinary material from which they are constructed. In relating this type of feature to a mass audience do you then borrow terms from popular culture?

O.I.: This type of communication does not just mean that you should refer to rock 'n roll or some other expression of popular fashion in too literal a sense. What I am pursuing now is the transformation of my architecture into a kind of medium in itself, so I do not have to design buildings but rather I design their medium.

C.K. and J.R.N.: This type of work can appear to be provocative and shocking. Are you really interested

in the design of such a "medium", or is it a statement of architectural sabotage?

O.I.: It's leaning more towards sabotage! [He smiles.] A characteristic of Buddhism is "dropping out", but in fact it implies more than this in that it signifies the act of becoming free and the meaning is therefore not a negative one. I feel that the importance of creating a new language in architecture is much greater than that of building ten ready-made commercial blocks.

C.K. and J.R.N.: In being provocative, it seems that subversion could become a whole new architectural category of its own.

O.I.: What is most important to me in architecture is to achieve freedom, therefore the expression of this freedom becomes the most problematic task. Luis Diez Del Corral, the Spanish philosopher wrote in his book, *Del Nuevo al Viejo Mundo*, that when he was flying at a height of ten thousand meters over India and saw a huge and impressive sunrise, he associated the experience with the state that Buddha had attained through meditation. In the philosopher's case the experience was achieved through aerodynamics. The Apollo astronauts similarly remarked that they had felt an almost religious kind of experience when they were free in space—this was achieved through "astro-technology." We can consider this type of experience as a proper expression of the relation between Buddhism and technology which we discussed earlier. Of course I realize that the possibilities of building construction are nothing in comparison with the high technology used in aviation and space exploration.

C.K. and J.R.N.: Do you hope that you might one day reach that state of euphoria through your architectural work?

O.I.: Architecture is not the best way of communicating such experiences, and therefore I write books. Maybe through writing I will be able to express some of this freedom.

C.K. and J.R.N.: What would you say are the strongest constraints or obstacles that still keep you from reaching that freedom?

O.I.: Nationalism is the major obstacle that I would like to overcome. As conservatism has strengthened in Japan it logically follows that its nationalism has as well. What I mean is real nationalism in its political sense; this is indeed a difficult obstacle to overcome.

Japan developed a protective attitude towards its industries, especially the building industry. Japan uses methods of protective commerce even for rice trading, and now the economy is getting weaker and weaker while a sense of nationalism expands.

C.K. and J.R.N.: But your own position isn't that controversial—you applaud Japanese craftsmanship and heritage.

O.I.: Of course, there appears some inherent contradiction in what I said but what I place a lot of critical attention on is the vast influence of Americanization in Japanese culture. This we have to overcome.

C.K. and J.R.N.: Whom can you call on for support in such a task?

O.I.: The support comes from people committed to media work, editors for example. One thing that must be realized is that the mainstream of Japanese architecture has always been extremely conservative.

C.K. and J.R.N.: How does the rejection of, or indifference to Americanization and conservatism and influence from the West in general, relate to Buddhism? Is it the desire to maintain a stable personal position?

O.I.: The idea is, as you said, somewhat connected to Buddhism. What is needed now from a historical viewpoint, is the development of a state of individualism, which has always been weak throughout Japanese history.

Amongst Equals

C.K. and J.R.N.: Having mentioned Macau and the Haishi Kaishi project, where do you situate your neighboring countries' influences on Japan's modern architectural scene?

O.I.: In Japan throughout the postwar years, the Western influence was so strong that it even managed to weaken Asian influences.

C.K. and J.R.N.: Do you think this impact will undermine Japan's recent superior architectural stance amongst its neighbors, and will its influence decline in comparison to that of Malaysia, Singapore, or Taiwan?

O.I.: It won't be Japanese architects who decline but all architects will become equal in their powers

of influence. This includes architects in Taiwan and Japan as well as European ones.

C.K. and J.R.N.: If Japan is so far removed from its roots, having opened itself up to strong Western influences, is it now slightly afraid that its Asian neighbors have developed more independently?

O.I.: No. What is happening now is that American architecture is having a great impact on Chinese architecture. It is not the case that China has evolved a new sense of Chinese architecture. Like Japan, China has somehow simply "rearranged" all the American architecture. It will now take quite a long time for China to establish a unique style of Chinese architecture.

Obsolete Architects

C.K. and J.R.N.: There are many ways of transporting architectural ideas abroad—through your books, exhibitions, the Internet and of course interviews. What is the most favorable image you have of yourself and that you would like to see exported?

O.I.: That of the outsider. Perhaps positioned somewhere outside the map that we mentioned earlier.

C.K. and J.R.N.: Outside your own map?

O.I.: It is not that I really want to be outside, but I am in fact outside for many reasons—my background, my family, and my teachers.

C.K. and J.R.N.: Who in your opinion is of particular influence from outside Japan?

O.I.: Many influential architects have come from abroad including Buckminster Fuller, Christopher Alexander, and Konrad Wachsmann. In Japan the mainstream was formed mainly by general contractors, big construction companies, and various amalgamations. I would like to see my position in line with other outsiders, namely my predecessors in architectural history.

C.K. and J.R.N.: In the scheme of Japanese architectural life, what aspect would you take credit for?

O.I.: I think that I have influenced the architectural world of Japan through the freedom that I have engaged in myself. But I would like to add that in ten years time I believe that architects will be extinct. Schools of architecture will be extinct as well.

Kazuo Shinohara

October 16, 1997

Kazuo Shinohara suggested the interview be held at the Centennial Hall of the Tokyo Institute of Technology (TIT), one of his best-known buildings. Following a lecture to foreign students on his life's work, the atmosphere among visitors and students alike was very animated.

The Shinohara School and Geometric Space

Christopher Knabe and Joerg Rainer Noennig: How did the name "Shinohara School" come about?

Kazuo Shinohara: That's quite hard to say, but the term can now be found in *Sir Banister Fletcher's A History of Architecture*.

C.K. and J.R.N.: Are you happy that people talk about the "Shinohara School", or do you have doubts about what they mean?

K.S.: Of course the definition of the Shinohara School isn't rigid; many architects and critics have used this term and it very often generates a positive response. It is also difficult to gauge how far its influence reaches or even if it is of interest. When I had an exhibition in Krems, a beautiful historical town about eighty kilometers west of Vienna on the river Danube former students came all the way from Barcelona and Paris. Other architects came from Berlin and Zurich for my lecture and symposium, one asking for information about members of the Shinohara School.

C.K. and J.R.N.: Many famous architects are associated with your school. How closely are they actually linked with it?

K.S.: For instance, Toyo Ito has been called a member of the school, but he wasn't a real member of my laboratory, while Itsuko Hasegawa in fact joined the Institute as a research student. Kazunari Sakamoto graduated from our Institute and is now a professor there.

C.K. and J.R.N.: Is it surprising for you that a younger generation of architects are also regarded as members of the Shinohara School? Kazuo Sejima is included in this group, but apparently she's never been part of your laboratory. What do you think those who are considered members of the Shinohara School have in common? Isn't there a peculiar style that might distinguish them?

K.S.: That's difficult to say; it's also hard to determine who should be included. Is there a relationship between my architectural concepts and

Tokyo Institute of Technology Centennial Hall, 1987. Above: view from southwest, below: cross-section.

methods and those of Sejima? What do you think about that? Is there a similarity, anything intellectual we might have in common, an architectural attitude, or something about our attention to detail?

C.K. and J.R.N.: In your works, there is a personal development that spans forty years, a steady progression towards your most recent abstract projects. In Sejima's case, she started off from quite an abstract level of thinking and architecture. Her style's most noticeable feature is the radicalism of her reduction and geometrical purity. Could this be enough of a characteristic to determine who belongs to the Shinohara School?

K.S.: Could Sejima's radicalism be a marker for those who belong to my school? Another marker is perhaps "geometry"? My main concept has always been space and its geometry [indicates the space of the Centennial Hall]. Let's take a look at this space here: it is not a simple space but a cube related to some oblique transformations; however at the top is inscribed an exact half-cylinder, which is a precise and simple geometric form.

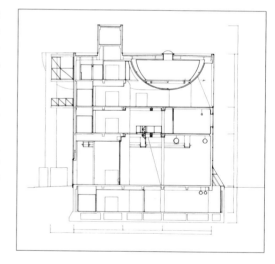

C.K. and J.R.N.: But the resulting space doesn't look simple at all. The geometry clearly forms the main expression in your buildings while the tactile factors are suppressed. It would be interesting to talk about the origins of your concepts, and the changes that have occurred in the considerable time you have been working with this pure, geometric space.

House in Kugayama,
1954. South elevation.

K.S.: My first work was the house in Kugayama in 1954. When the project was described in an English magazine, the editor wrote that Mies van der Rohe and the Katsura Detached Palace in Kyoto had influenced the work. This is quite accurate, so precisely objective. At that time, just after World War II, Tokyo had been completely destroyed, and building materials were of poor quality and very hard to obtain. If in those days the main architectural trend had been a sort of postmodernist style, we simply couldn't have followed it because we lacked the materials it required. Fortunately, the trend was towards modern Minimalism. From Mies van der Rohe's architecture, which of course has many other aspects to it, we could abstract some form of Minimalism.

C.K. and J.R.N.: And the Minimalism of Mies had its roots in tradition, particularly in the Classicism of the German architect Karl Friedrich Schinkel. From him Mies developed his sense of order and aesthetics.

K.S.: Yes, this is an important issue behind our Minimalism: the background for Mies' architecture and Japanese architecture are quite different.

C.K. and J.R.N.: Minimalism and Modernism seem to coincide in your case. Obviously it was a tremendous job to develop a Japanese Modernism away from any classical European influence. However, yet another version of Modernism came via Kenzo Tange and Kunio Maekawa to Japan from Le Corbusier—who was not a minimalist.

K.S.: In the 1950s, we assumed Mies van der Rohe to be a pure minimalist, not recognizing his fundamentally different background from our own. Paul Rudolph, who died, had visited Tokyo in the 1960s and Fumihiko Maki and I met him to discuss certain issues. He mentioned the Katsura Detached Palace, but it didn't appear to excite him; yet not long before, Walter Gropius had visited Katsura Detached Palace and he, by contrast, was fascinated by it.

C.K. and J.R.N.: The understanding of Modernism had already changed. Paul Rudolph, a strong second generation modernist couldn't appreciate the same features as Gropius, who might be called a co-inventor of Modernism, together with Mies and Le Corbusier.

K.S.: Yes, in my case, the concept of Modernism was influenced by way of Mies van der Rohe. In 1950, he built the Farnsworth Residence, and this was our starting point; we couldn't look to his earlier works. In this way we left behind those heavy, rigid structures of his early houses. At that time, I clearly remember Rudolph explaining the Farnsworth Residence. Mies' intention wasn't the "post and beam" structure; his main concept was to enclose space by glass walls, to make a glass cube.

Filtering Modernism

C.K. and J.R.N.: Unlike many Japanese architects at the time, you didn't travel to Europe to study Modernism. Your first trip abroad was in 1972, and thereafter you reduced Modernism to a more conceptual level.

K.S.: That's right, the Japanese understanding of Modernism in the 1950s actually developed from America and not only from Europe. The American one was more pragmatic.

C.K. and J.R.N.: By this time the ideology of Modernism was significantly altered and much in question: it became a problematic matter, but the options and the opportunities of modern space weren't yet fully exploited.

Would it be fair to say that your work was an attempt at "filtering" Modernism in an aesthetic sense?

K.S.: In the 1950s many architects of my age [in their thirties] were adherents of Modernism, and - followed Rationalism and Functionalism, but I didn't. I rigidly concentrated on tradition, intentionally focusing on Japanese history, although Mies inspired my early work of course. The Katsura Palace was a villa belonging to the Imperial family and therefore very impressive, but I switched my attention to more ordinary people's houses after my first work. I called this new work "vernacular". My main concepts were neither Functionalism nor Rationalism, despite their importance. Too many young architects bandied such terms about. *Shoin* [traditional type of residence for aristocrats and warriors], including Katsura Detached Palace, was my basic interest, of course.

C.K. and J.R.N.: You have devoted many years to linking Japanese tradition to Modernism. Do you think that other young architects wanted to achieve "instant Modernism", and in doing so almost lost their way?

K.S.: Possibly so. And now after Postmodernism, it has become the trend to use the word Modernism again and indeed to invent a "new Modernism". This is true for many architects in Japan. European architects take up the same word but theirs is derived from the original whilst ours is still a selective usage.

Impacts

C.K. and J.R.N.: Where do young Japanese architects draw their inspiration from today?

K.S.: At present I'm pursuing a series of conversations in *Kenchiku Gijutsu* [*Architecture Technology*], a more engineering-orientated journal. In this series younger architects sometimes mention Swiss architects.

C.K. and J.R.N.: They've achieved an enormous level of popularity in Japan indeed. These Swiss architects are also minimalist, but unlike the rational Modernists of the 1920s they don't focus on engineering aspects or on technology. Le Corbusier admired the "machine", but more recent Minimalism departs from a different point, and it has begun to incorporate artistic concepts too.

K.S.: I recently participated at a conference on future architecture in Krems. A former Austrian student of mine, Ernst Beneder, now active in Vienna as an architect, organized the event. On the first day we discussed "Movement in Space" and "Transitional Space". The second day was about "Topos" and the third day was devoted to "Metropolis". There weren't only architects present but people from related fields, such as philosophers and even politicians, but surprisingly, technology and industry were not the main issues.

First and Second Styles:
Japanese Tradition and the Cube

C.K. and J.R.N.: Do you think such theoretical discourse has a greater impact on European architects than your built designs?

K.S.: In 1979 I had my first exhibition in France. On the question of practice, the architect–engineer, Mr. Noriaki Okabe, was well acquainted with my work and concepts, especially during the time he was in Paris. Naturally, French architects have appreciated my theory, but Mr. Okabe believes that my design work has had more direct impact than my theory. At the last Krems symposium in Austria, a young Japanese, Ms. Mie Goto, who had been living there for some time, explained that my concepts aren't entirely understood there, although my work

House in White, 1966. South elevation.

is well known. Space, and architecture itself, always seems to have a greater and more direct impact than the theories that surround them.

C.K. and J.R.N.: Yes, your buildings certainly express your ideas more clearly than any writing could. Looking at them, it is possible to trace your intellectual development from the first stage of your design, which is your "traditional style". You wrote your graduation thesis on the theme of tradition. The House in White [1966] resembles the thirteenth-century Jodo-ji temple. You didn't stick to this first style.

K.S.: No, I didn't. Just as I feel that I am beginning to reach a starting point, or way of working, my mind begins to focus on a different direction. Once I had made the decision to leave off investigating tradition, having defined it as my first style, it necessarily implied that a second style would follow!

C.K. and J.R.N.: How long did this second style take to develop? And what was its most important feature?

K.S.: It was quite a short period, around five years. One clear condition was the cube shape which developed from my ideas about space as I'd expressed them in the House in White. The floor space of the cube was ten square meters, with 6.4 square meters of living space, and a height of 3.6 meters. It was a very pure and minimal space. Admittedly, Modernism's basic framework is the cube too, but I hadn't intended pursuing this framework which so many architects of the 1950s and 1960s had done before me. So when I use the word "cube", it's in a sense that developed from my own interpretation of space.

C.K. and J.R.N.: What distinguishes your theory from the other dominant stream in recent Japanese architecture, the one begun by Kenzo Tange and continued by Arata Isozaki? After your "cube" period, you tackled Rationalism conceptually: you set up the theories of "savagery" and "noise" in order to imply a degree of irrationality. At the same time Isozaki criticized Rationalism by introducing the curves of Marilyn Monroe into his architecture.

K.S.: One type of architect in Japan, the so called "progressive architect", largely engages with Western concepts and is adept at taking these Western models on board. At first, such architects dealt with Modernism, then Postmodernism and now some of them are talking about Neo-Modernism—and are therefore always up to date. I, on the other hand, abstracted the form of expression using a cube, but the exact base must still be sought in my own process.

C.K. and J.R.N.: What characteristics of the cube were you searching for?

K.S.: The meaning Le Corbusier placed on space and background is different from mine. Le Corbusier and Mies freed and extracted the cube from traditional entrenched ideas. I abstracted traditional Japanese architecture in the House in White, and this I did step by step. Five years later I wanted to change my style again. Tradition is my first style and the cube is the second. Naturally the third style had to differ from the first two. This started with the Tanikawa House [1974] and incorporated neither tradition nor the cube.

The Third Style: Human Machines

C.K. and J.R.N.: So the cube disappeared and with the Tanikawa House you developed a space which was less unified but more complex. Does this hold true for your current work?

K.S.: Now I'm working in my fourth style, but I can never tell whether I will succeed.

C.K. and J.R.N.: Your intentions are obviously well communicated; in the House in White an historical aura makes itself felt while the Centennial Hall has been seen as a comic book hero by local children.

K.S.: When the Centennial Hall was finished, the kids actually named it Gun-dam, which is a cartoon character, an urban robot hero. What an interesting reaction to the building.

C.K. and J.R.N.: It certainly looks like a machine.

K.S.: It really is! It's not a "hard" machine as it contains a lot of humanity. In the same way the Japanese children's animation character, Gun-dam, is regarded as having quite human attributes. The children's response fulfilled my intention.

C.K. and J.R.N.: What did you do after that building?

K.S.: The majority of my projects had been for houses, but the scale has changed dramatically now. Before this building, the Ukiyoe Museum [1982] in

Matsumoto was the biggest of my works Yet it is only a third the size of the Centennial Hall. The next work, K2 in Osaka, was three times as big as that, and the Euralille hotel project is three times the size of K2!

Obstacles:
The Euralille, Helsinki, and Yokohama projects

C.K. and J.R.N.: What has happened to your Euralille design?

K.S.: My first version was nominated for realization and included in the Euralille Exhibition in Paris in 1990. It received the strong support of Rem Koolhaas, master planner for the scheme, and was also promoted by Euralille itself. My later version satisfied all their specific conditions. Sadly the budget was insufficient. I was subsequently asked to revise the design, and Euralille fully expected to realize this simplified scheme that incorporates an oblique fissure. The cost calculations for this project were almost feasible. But right at this time, in fall 1992, misfortune struck the French economy and the project came under threat. Yet they still wanted me to participate in the project on a reduced scale. The "spatial envelope" was reduced by half of the original. I couldn't get too excited about this design in the light of the problems posed by the economic situation, so I quit the project in the end. A local architect undertook to design the project at this reduced scale but failed to gain support for his work. The director informs me that he still dreams of realizing the original version.

C.K. and J.R.N.: Today your work has become very popular. Yet your earlier works were rather esoteric pieces—almost exercises in personal exploration. Was there any difficulty in dealing with your new, more widespread popularity?

K.S.: There was certainly a kind of popularity, but it was not that widespread. Some of my projects are as yet unrealized. I entered the Helsinki Museum of Modern Art competition but the design wasn't pursued. I designed a certain room in the permanent exhibition space, where the judges felt access would have been a little difficult. I'd made a wide platform that sloped slightly to the north and was open; the judge said that such a "void" could only be used in summer. I thought if people were able to use the space in summer that would be fine. In other seasons this space could simply be looked at—isn't that enough? Admittedly my general concepts are very difficult to understand, but the judge used the number of elevators as his reason for rejecting the work! For me, this was a minor technical problem—easily adjustable. So you can see that my projects aren't popular with everybody.

C.K. and J.R.N.: A similar case was the Yokohama Port Terminal competition; in the first rounds of selection your design was favored, but then one judge claimed the project was too monumental, and that it would be unsuitable for the site because of its symbolism.

K.S.: Yes. This was largely owing to one postmodernist. Maybe he was afraid of having this work realized. The judges could easily recognize who'd designed it even at this early stage. He used such a poor and ugly logic to exclude my work, saying it was too symbolic for the site! Afterwards I met a certain professor in Vienna who's a little older than me, and he told me frankly that he could easily understand my earlier projects, but had difficulty in following my fourth style. When he looked at the Yokohama scheme, he must have recognized the continuity of my work.

White Noise and the F14 Tomcat jet fighter

C.K. and J.R.N.: What kind of work are you engaged in currently?

K.S.: Last year I had a very serious illness. After that I concentrated mostly on finishing a new book. I don't feel the need to do much practical architectural work at the moment so I put my effort into writing. The first book I wrote back in 1964, was entitled *House Design*. Perhaps the current one will be the last; it's based on urbanism. I started from the concept of the house, while carrying out separate studies on Tokyo and urbanism. At some point these interests crossed; I think this must have coincided with the period of my third style. Now my ambition is to analyze Tokyo and its divers phenomena. I actually began the study back in the 1960s, but at

that time my building designs were quite independent from my ideas about the metropolis. Now I have to work out the connection between them. I may say that the concept of my small houses and my recent interest in the city are connected at their roots, although they weren't visibly linked for twenty years. In the House in Uehara [1976] these concepts probably coincide visually for the first time.

C.K. and J.R.N.: In your first house designs there were no notable references to Tokyo. Only in the 1970s you introduced the "fissure" as an important spatial element in your designs, as a crevice that bisects the cubes. This fragmented notion of a space is essential in Tokyo. Nowadays your architecture clearly responds to the city since you've overlapped the concepts developed in the 1980s, the "Zero Degree Machine" and "Progressive Anarchy". Can we say that the first arises out of a more architectural scope while the second emerges directly from Tokyo's urban landscape?

K.S.: If I were an architect in Vienna or Paris, I'd never have come up with such a concept or developed real projects from it, even if I'd thought deeply about these metropolises. The conditions surrounding my concepts are peculiar to Japan. At a certain point I began to take a genuine interest in Tokyo and I developed a real appreciation for this city. Nobody else could stand Tokyo: they all wanted to change the city as Le Corbusier had hoped to do in Paris with his controversial project La Ville Radieuse. One of the representative groups for this stream were the Metabolists. Tange developed his Tokyo Bay project.

C.K. and J.R.N.: Isozaki worked in Tange's studio at that time and about then developed his "City in the Air" project more or less in the center of Tokyo. Significantly the city underneath his cluster of high-rises wasn't described and he simply ignored it. You, on the contrary, tried to discover the positive aspect in Tokyo's "progressive anarchy". It took a long time, however, to find beauty in the chaos of Tokyo and to abstract a sort of compositional principle from it. You have referred to the Tomcat jet fighter airplane as a metaphor which features the perfect connection of completely disparate parts.

K.S.: I used the F14 [US Navy Tomcat jet fighter] as a positive example because each part of this machine is designed for a precise function and is,

House in Uehara, Tokyo, 1976. View from living room to children's room.

therefore, independent in shape. They are not intended to harmonize or create any sense of unity at all as in the elegant ocean liners of the 1920s! And in this respect we can regard Tokyo as similar to the F14, or discuss the functions of a house in the same manner. In the Tomcat fighter each part realizes its absolute function. Tokyo isn't quite as efficient, but to a degree it is still close to the definition of white noise, namely something that contains many frequencies at equal intensities. Similarly each part of Tokyo functions, not perfectly, but somehow it works. It is noisy—but not a bad sound at all.

Tokyo's Progressive Anarchy

K.S.: All over Tokyo and indeed the whole of Japan, you can see electrical wires and transformers above the streets. These are often cited as symbols of Tokyo's ugliness. Artists and architects advocate putting them underground to tidy up the streets, if only this were possible. But I doubt the country could ever afford it. The wires are now a characteristic part of Tokyo and are there mostly for economic reasons.

C.K. and J.R.N.: Architecture must always be able to react to the given conditions, and you've proved this is possible in the House under High Voltage Wires, where you "sliced" the building according to the easement regulations.

K.S.: That's right, but who can eliminate these conditions? I have faced them in a *sachlich* posture. When an architect, one of the organizers of my Vienna exhibition, first arrived in Tokyo, she felt overwhelmed by the number of wires overhead. After a few days she had become indifferent to them.

C.K. and J.R.N.: A "Tokyo style" certainly seems to exist and this is dispersed, by degree, throughout Japan. Toyo Ito for instance, came up with his principles of "Filter Architecture" as a way of abstracting elements. This method might well be applied to Tokyo since it is impossible to conceive of the city as a whole, but it is possible to "filter" elements of its enormous reality into something concrete and awe-inspiring.

K.S.: Tokyo is too vast to tackle in its entirety. Even if some mighty fascist architect appeared in Tokyo and tried to change the look of the city completely, he could hardly succeed because of the huge number of structures and their diversity, from the smallest shacks to the various commercial blocks. Furthermore there are many legal conditions concerning building that have to be satisfied. Whenever building on an existing street I've always run into unforeseeable problems, not only legal matters but also aesthetic ones. While your building goes up, some of the existing structures will remain, others will be demolished or altered, but you don't know which ones or when. Unfortunately you don't have the chance to give everything a face-lift. Urban conditions in Tokyo are notoriously unstable, so an architect's vision, like that of early Modernism, has its limits.

C.K. and J.R.N.: Why would anyone even want to manipulate Tokyo in terms of a master plan? Surely they'd need a Metabolist approach, for example the method of Tange's master plan for Tokyo Bay. But this understanding of the metropolis is certainly outdated — it is after all thirty years old.

K.S.: If an architect collaborates with politicians or has good connections he may be able to realize projects like Tange's master-plan for Tokyo. I just find that type of approach boring by comparison with places whose aesthetic is harmonized into the existing city. My opinion is supported by my work. Vienna and Paris contain areas of beauty that are sufficient and there is no need to interfere with the entire scheme; similarly I think that Tokyo has its own kind of given, or existing, beauty.

Mathematical Design

C.K. and J.R.N.: The aesthetic of Tokyo is certainly reflected in your most recent projects. For instance the colliding shapes of the Centennial Hall present a kind of fragmentation that you might have derived from Tokyo's cityscape, and this is also reflected in the mathematics of the building. You, in fact, separated the building into two parts in order to calculate the statics independently.

K.S.: The calculation itself was of great interest to me because the mathematical methods are similar to my design process. Even though our Institute's super computers can resolve around three thousand equations at a time, it was still a complex task. The engineers, Mr. Akira Wada and Toshihiko Kimura, separated the structure into two parts in order to calculate them independently. Thereafter we had to pursue solutions by combining the results for both volumes. By asymptotic method they approximated the influences.

C.K. and J.R.N.: It is characteristic of your architecture that, although the overall form develops from a complex shape, the structural system can still be treated logically and rationally. You tend to use various primary forms and articulate their collision. The Kumamoto Police Station features various structural systems that aren't coherent, but form different sections and partitions.

K.S.: Although the Kumamoto structures are not as complicated as the Centennial Hall, the basic concept isn't that different.

House under High Voltage Wires, 1981. View from northwest.

Kumamoto-Kita Police Station, Kumamoto, 1991. View from northwest.

Finding Oneself

C.K. and J.R.N.: Like a modernist's search for "truth" in architecture, is such correspondence between function and structure as in the Kumamoto-Kita Police Headquarters intended to be an expression of "architectural truth"? Do you feel you have developed further than the modernists in this respect?

K.S.: Take for instance the Yokohama Port Terminal project. This wasn't a very complicated shape. Its planning algorithm didn't start with a set of functions to be juxtaposed and integrated; in general the design was clear and simple. In Yokohama it was not necessary to realize complexity. There is just the ocean, that speaks for itself.

C.K. and J.R.N.: One point asserted by the panel of judges about your Yokohama project was its special beauty. It's no exaggeration to claim the same for all your works. Beauty seems a particular goal in all of your previous projects: first the Japanese aesthetic

followed by the modernist; then, finally, the beauty inherent in chaotic Tokyo.

K.S.: What should come after that? It is very difficult to decide, myself. On the last day of the symposium at the Krems exhibition, I asked the audience what they thought and whether they had found a new direction for the future. People said they'd been surprised by my works. After the symposium an architect came up to me and said: "You have already succeeded in showing us new directions in future architecture by your buildings. Why are you so keen to find a new way?" Then, he added: "You're already the master of Japan. Why are you still thinking about new directions?".

C.K. and J.R.N.: Did you answer him?

K.S.: No. Of course I greatly appreciated his comments, but it's not easy to respond. I could have replied that I was sure I'd find another new direction, but it wouldn't have been honest. It is difficult for me; it may or may not be possible. Now it's time to move on and to explore further.

Biographies

TADAO ANDO
ARCHITECT & PLANNER

TADAO ANDO ARCHITECT & ASSOCIATES
5-23. TOYOSAKI 2-CHOME. KITA-KU. OSAKA JAPAN 〒531 PHONE 06(375)1148

安藤忠雄

安藤忠雄建築研究所
〒531 大阪市北区豊崎2丁目5-23 PHONE.06(375)1148

Tadao Ando

1941	Born in Osaka.
1962–69	Traveled though Europe, USA, and Africa; self-education in architecture.
Since 1969	Private practice in Osaka.
1997	Professor at the University of Tokyo.

Principal Works

1976	Townhouses (Azuma House), Osaka.
1977–78	Glass Block House (Ishihara House), Osaka.
1979–81	Koshino House, Hyogo.
1982–86	Kidosaki House, Tokyo.
1983	Rokko Apartments, Kobe.
1985–93	Rokko Apartments II, Kobe.
1985–88	Galleria (Akka), Osaka.
1985–87	Kara-za Mobile Theater.
1986	Chapel on Mount Rokko, Kobe.
1984/91	Time's Buildings I & II, Kyoto.
1987–89	Children's Museum, Hyogo.
1988	Church on the Water.
1989	Church with the Light, Osaka.
1989	RAIKA Headquarters, Osaka.
1989–93	Vitra Conference Pavilion, Weil am Rhein.
1991	Water Temple, Awaji Hyogo.
1992	Japanese Pavilion, Seville Expo.
1997–	Modern Art Museum of Fort Worth.

Awards

1979	Annual Prize of the Architectural Institute of Japan for townhouse (Azuma House).
1983	Japanese Cultural Design Prize for Rokko Housing.
1984	Alvar Aalto Medal of the Finnish Association of Architects.
1987	Mainichi Art Prize for Chapel on Mount Rokko.
1988	Isoya Yoshida Award for Kidosaki House.
1989	Médaille d'or de l'Académie d'Architecture, France.
1991	Art Prize of Osaka.
1992	Carlsberg Prize for Architecture, Denmark.

東京大学名誉教授　　原　広司

東京都渋谷区鉢山町10-3
Tel. 03 - 3464 - 8670

Hiroshi Hara

1936	Born in Kawasaki, Japan.
1959	University of Tokyo, B.A.
1961	University of Tokyo, M.A.
1964	University of Tokyo, Ph.A., Associate Professor at Faculty of Architecture, University of Tokyo.
1969	Associate Professor at Institute of Industrial Science, University of Tokyo.
1970	Collaborates with Atelier for Design Practices.
1982	Professor at Institute of Industrial Science, University of Tokyo.
1997	Professor Emeritus University of Tokyo.

Principal Works

1968	Keisho Kindergarten, Machida, Tokyo.
1972	Awazu House, Kawasaki, Kanagawa.
1974	Hara House, Machida, Tokyo.
1980	Sueda Art Gallery, Yufuin, Oita.
1981	"The Stage of Dreams", Nakatsuka House lto, Shizuoka.
1986	Tasaki Museum of Art, Karuizawa, Nagano.
1986	Yamato International, Ota-ku, Tokyo.
1987	Josei Primary School, Naha, Okinawa.
1988	Iida City Museum, Iida, Nagano.
1992	Ose Middle School Uchiko, Ehime.

1993	Umeda Sky Building, Kita-ku, Osaka.
1997	Kyoto Station Buiiding, Sakyo-ku, Kyoto.
1998	Miyagi Prefectural Library, Sendai, Miyagi.

Awards

1986	Annual Award of the Architectural Institute of Japan for Tasaki Museum of Art.
1987	Media Park KoIn International Urban Design Competition (one of six winners).
1987	Naha City Townscape Award for Josei Primary School.
1988	1st Togo Murano Award for Yamato International.
1988	Suntory Award for "Space 'From Function to Modality'"(book).
1989	The Central Districts Architectural Award for Iida City Museum.
1990	La Cité International de Montréal, Montreal 1990–2000/International Competition in Urban Design and Urban Planning (one of three winners).
1993	Nikkei BP Technology Award Grand Prize for Umeda Sky Building.

ITSUKO
HASEGAWA

Itsuko Hasegawa Atelier
1-9-7 Yushima Bunkyo-Ku
Tokyo 113 Japan
TEL:03-3818-5470
FAX:03-3818-4381

長谷川逸子

長谷川逸子・建築計画工房
113 東京都文京区湯島1-9-7
TEL:03-3818-5470
FAX:03-3818-4381

Itsuko Hasegawa

1964	Graduated from Department of Architecture, Kanto Gakuin University.
1964–69	Worked in office of Kiyonori Kikutake.
1969–71	Research student in Department of Architecture, Tokyo Institute of Technology.
1971–78	Worked as an assistant to Kazuo Shinohara Atelier in Tokyo Institute of Technology.
1979	Established ltsuko Hasegawa Atelier.
1988–90	Lecturer at Waseda University.
1990–92	Lecturer at Tokyo Institute of Technology.
1992–93	Visiting Professor at Harvard University Graduate School of Design.
1997	Hon. FRIBA.

Principal Works

1979	Tokumaru Childrens' Clinic.
1980	House at Kuwahara, Matsuyama.
1982	Aono Building.
1984	NC House.
1984	Bizan Hall.
1985	BY House.
1986	Sugai Hospital, Matsuyama.
1989	Nagoya Design Expo Interior Pavilion.
1990	Shiranui Hospital Stress-Care Center.
1990	Shonandai Cultural Center.
1990	Cona Village.
1991	Kindergarten at Midorigaoka, Atsugi.
1991	S.T.M. House.
1991	Footwork Computer Center.
1991	Busshoji Elementary School, Himi.
1994	Sumida Culture Factory.
1994	Oshima-Machi Picture Book Museum.
1995	Yamanashi Fruit Garden.
1995	Himi Seaside Botanical Garden, Himi.
1996	Kaiho Elementary School, Himi.

Awards

1986	Architectural Institute of Japan Prize for Design (Bizan Hall).
1986	First Prize, Open Competition for Shonandai Cultural Center, Fujisawa.
1986	Japan Cultural Design Award.
1989	First Prize, Invited Competition for the Urban Scape in Shiogama.
1990	Avon Arts Award.
1990	First Prize, Invited Competition for Sumida Culture Center, Tokyo.
1992	BCS Prize for Shonandai Cultural Center, Fujisawa.
1992	First Prize, Hospital Architecture Award (Shiranui Hospital, Stress-Care Center).
1993	First Prize, Proposal Competition of Niigata City Cultural Hall and Area Development.
1995	First Prize, Proposal Competition of Kurahashi-Machi Town Center Development.

OSAMU ISHIYAMA
architect

Professor of Architectural School
WASEDA UNIVERSITY
3-4-1 Okubo, Shinjuku-ku, Tokyo 169-8555 JAPAN
Tel: 03-3209-2278 Fax: 03-3209-8944

石山 修武
早稲田大学教授

早稲田大学理工学部建築学科
東京都新宿区大久保3-4-1 〒169-8555
TEL.03-3209-2278 FAX.03-3209-8944

ARATA ISOZAKI

Arata Isozaki & Associates
TEL 03-3405-1526
FAX 03-3475-5265
9-6-17 Akasaka,Minato-ku
Tokyo, 107 Japan

磯 崎 新

Arata Isozaki & Associates

株式会社 磯崎 新 アトリエ
TEL (03)3405-1526
FAX (03)3475-5265
東京都港区赤坂9-6-17 〒107

Osamu Ishiyama

1944   Born in Tokyo.
1966   Graduated from Waseda University,
        Department of Architecture.
1968   Finished graduate studies at Waseda
        University.
1985   Awarded the Tenth Yoshida Prize
        for his work on the Izu Chohachi
        Museum.
1988   Began work as professor at Waseda
        University's Department of Architecture.
1995   Received the Design Award from the
        Architectal Institute of Japan for his
        work on the Rias Ark Museum.

Arata Isozaki

1931   Born in Oita City.
1954   Graduated from Architectural Faculty
        of University of Tokyo.
1963   Established Arata Isozaki &
        Associates
1983   Juror of the Peak International
        Architectural Competition.

1986   Juror of the Architectural Competi-
        tion for The New National Theater
        of Japan by Ministry of Construction,
        Japan.
1988-98 Commissioner of Kumamoto Artpolis.
1988   Juror of the Design Competition for the
        Passenger Terminal Building of the
        Kansai International Airport.
1991   Juror of the International Architect's
        Competition for EXPO '95 in Vienna.
1991   Juror of the International Competition
        for the Kyoto Station Building.
1991-92 General Commissioner of Visions
        of Japan exhibition, Japan Festival,
        London.
1995   Juror of Yokohama International Port
        Terminal Design Competition,
        Yokohama, Japan.

Principal Works

1959-60 Oita Medical Hall, Oita, Japan; 1970-72
        Annex.
1962-66 Oita Prefectural Library, Oita, Japan.
1966-67 Fukuoka City Bank, Oita Branch, Oita,
        Japan.
1966-70 Expo '70 Festival Plaza, Osaka, Japan.
1968-71 Fukuoka City Bank, Head Office,
        Fukuoka, Japan.
1971-74 The Museum of Modern Art, Gunma,
        Japan.
1972-74 Kita-kyushu City Museum of Art,
        Fukuoka, Japan.
1973-74 Kita-kyushu Central Library, Fukuoka,
        Japan.
1976-78 Kamioka Town Hall, Gifu, Japan.
1978-79 Space-Time in Japan "MA", Exhibition
        Festival d'Automne à Paris, France.

1978–83	Tsukuba Center Building, Ibaragi, Japan.
1981–86	The Museum of Contemporary Art, Los Angeles, U.S.A.
1983–90	Palau D' Esports Sant Jordi, Barcelona, Spain.
1986–90	Art Tower Mito, Ibaragi, Japan.
1986–93	Tokyo University of Art and Design, Tokyo, Japan.
1986–	The New Brooklyn Museum, New York, U.S.A.
1987–89	Bond University Administration/ Library/Humanities, Gold Coast, Queensland, Australia.
1987–90	Team Disney Building, Florida, U.S.A.
1987–96	Pabillón Polideportibo Palafolls, Spain.
1990–94	The Center of Japanese Art and Technology in Krakow, Poland.
1991–92	The Guggenheim Museum SoHo, New York, U.S.A.
1991–94	Nagi Museum of Contemporary Art, Okayama, Japan.
1991–95	Toyonokuni Libraries for Cultural Resources, Oita, Japan.
1991–95	Kyoto Concert Hall, Kyoto, Japan.
1991–95	B-con Plaza, Oita, Japan.
1992–98	Nara Convention Hall, Nara, Japan.
1993–95	DOMUS: La Casa del Hombre (Interactive Museum about Humankind), La Corufia, Spain.
1993–98	Higashi Shizuoka Cultural Complex Project, Shizuoka, Japan.
1995–98	Akiyoshidai International Arts Village, Yamaguchi, Japan.
1996	Biennale di Firenze '96, Time and Fashion, Italy.

Awards

1966	Annual Prize, Architectural Institute of Japan (Oita Prefectural Library).
1969	Artist's Newcomer Prize, Ministry of Culture (Fukuoka City Bank, Gita Branch.
1974	Annual Prize, Architectural Institute of Japan (The Museum of Modern Art, Gunma).
1983	Mainichi Art Award (Tsukuba Center Building).
1986	RIBA's Royal Gold Medal for Architecture (England).
1988	Arnold W.Brunner Memorial Prize of the American Academy and Institute of Arts and Letters.
1988	Asahi Award of the Asahi Shinbun.
1990	Chicago Architecture Award.

1992	Honor Award, the American Institute of Architects.
1994	RIBA Honorary Fellow, England.
1994	Royal Academy of Arts, Honorary Academician, England.
1996	Leone d'ore (Venice Biennale, commissioner of Japanese Pavilion).
1997	Gran Cruz de Ia Orden del Mérito Civil, Spain.
1997	Officier de L'Ordre des Arts et des Lettres, France.
1998	American Academy of Arts and Letters (Honorary Member).

ARCHITECT
TOYO ITO

TOYO ITO ARCHITECT & ASSOCIATES
1-19-4 Shibuya, Shibuya-ku, Tokyo, 150-0002, Japan
Phone 03-3409-5061, 3409-5822, Fax 03-3409-5969

代表取締役
株式会社 伊東豊雄建築設計事務所
東京都渋谷区渋谷1-19-4 不二屋ビル
電話・(代) 3409-5822 (直) 3409-5061 FAX3409-5969
伊東豊雄
〒150-0002

Toyo Ito

1941	Born in Japan.
1965	Graduated Tokyo University, department of architecture.
1965–69	Worked at Kiyonon Kikutake Architect and Associates.
1971	Started his own studio, Urban Robot (URBOT) in Tokyo.
1979	Studio changed its name to Toyo Ito and Associates, Architects.

Principal Works

1971	Aluminum House, Kanagawa.
1974	Cottage in Sengataki.
1975	"Black Recurrence".
1976	House in Nakano, "White U", Tokyo House in Kamiwada.
1977	Hotel D, Nagano.
1978	PMT Building in Nagoya, Aichi.
1979	PMT Building in Hakata, Fukuoka. PMT Factory in Osaka, Osaka. House in Koganei, Tokyo. House in Chuorinkan, Kanagawa.
1981	House in Kasama, Ibaragi.
1982	House in Umegaoka, Tokyo.
1983	House in Hanakoganei, Tokyo House in Denenchofu, Tokyo.
1984	Silver Hut, house of the architect, Tokyo.
1985	Project for the exhibition "Pao as Dwelling of Tokyo Nomad Women".
1986	House in Magomezawa, Chiba. Project for the exhibition "Furniture for Tokyo Nomad Women". Restaurant Nomad. Tower of Winds in Yokohama, Yokohama.
1987	M Building in Kanda, Tokyo.
1988	House in Takagicho, Tokyo.
1989	Guest House for Sapporo Beer Brewery, Hokkaido Restaurant Pastina. I Building in Asakusabashi, Tokyo.
1990	T Building in Nakameguro, Tokyo. Competition project "La Maison de la Culture de Japon à Paris". Rejuvenation project for the City of Antwerp.
1991	Yatsushiro Municipal Museum, Kumamoto. Lighting design for Opera House in Frankfurt. Gallery LI in Yugawara, Kanagawa. Gate of Okawabata River City 21, "Egg of Winds", Tokyo. F Building in Minamiaoyama, Tokyo. Hotel P, Hokkaido.
1992	Urban design project for Shanghai Luijiazui Central Area.
1993	Eckenheim Municipal Kindergarten, Frankfurt. ITM Building in Matsuyama, Ehime. Amusement Complex H, Tokyo. Shimosuwa Municipal Museum, Nagano 1994. Old People's Home in Yatsushiro, Kumamoto. Tsukuba South Parking Building, Ibaragi.
1995	Fire Station in Yatsushiro, Kumamoto. S House in Tateshina, Nagano.
1996	L Hall in Nagaoka, Niigata. S House in Oguni, Oita.
1997	Proposal for expansion project of MoMA. Community Center and Day Care Center in Yokohama. 0 Dome in Odate. Proposal for Seoul Dome competition 1998. Ota-ward Resort Complex Project, Nagano.

Awards

Hon., FAIA
Honorary Professor of University
of North London.

1979	First prize of nominated competition for Japan Airlines Ticket Counter.
1984	3rd Japan Architects Association award for House of Kasama.
1986	Architectural Institute of Japan award for "Silver Hut". First prize of nominated competition for The Tower of Yokohama.
1987	Japan Interior Designers Association award for "Nomad" and others.
1988	First prize of nominated competition for lighting of Frankfurt Opera House, Germany. First prize of nominated competition for 89 ARTEC Nagoya Biennale Pavilion.
1990	Togo Murano award for Sapporo Brewery Guest House.
1991	Kumamoto View Award for Yatsushiro Municipal Museum.
1992	33rd Mainichi Art Award for Yatsushiro Municipal Museum.
1993	BCS award for Yatsushiro Municipal Museum. First prize of nominated competition for Art and Cultural Hall Project in Nagaoka. First prize of nominated competition for Taishacho Municipal Cultural Hall.
1994	First prize of nominated competition for Otaward Resort Complex.
1995	First prize of competition for Mediathèque Project in Sendai. First prize of nominated competition for Agricultural Park in Oita.
1996	Invited to the proposal competition for Aquarium in Shimonoseki. Invited to the proposal competition for City Hall in Notsuharu, Oita.

1996	Kumamoto View Award for Yatsushiro Fire Station.
1997	Invited to the proposal competition for MoMA.
	IAA "INTERACH '97" Grand Prix of the Union of Architects in Bulgaria Gold Medal.
1998	Education Minister's Art Encouragement Prize in Japan.

Publications

1981	Translation of *The Mathematics of The Ideal Villa and Other Essays* by Colin Rowe.
1986	*Toyo Ito – Kaze no Henyotai [Transfiguration of Winds]*, Kajima Institute.
1997	*Nakano Honcho no Ie Sumai no Toshokan.*

began his design career in his twenties, winning an international competition of architecture design. Today much of his work can be seen worldwide.

His architecture and urban design are often inspired by literature and fine art, taking motifs from poems by Stéphane Mallarmé, Lautréamont, and others. His first stage set design in 1998, a recomposition of architectural elements from another context, was very successful. (*One of a kind*, by the Netherlands Dance Theater, first performed at Den Haag, Holland, afterwards at Vienna, Berlin, Paris, and elsewhere.)

Kitagawara is also known for his designs in the areas of furniture and decorative arts.

Kengo Kuma

Kuma was born in Kanagawa, Japan in 1954. He completed his Masters degree at Tokyo University in 1979 and was visiting scholar at Columbia University from 1985 to 1986. In 1987 he established Spatial Design Studio, and in 1990, Kengo Kuma & Associates. From 1994 he was a visiting critic at Columbia University. Among his major works are the Kirosan Observatory (1995), Water/Glass, for which he received the AIA Benedictus Award, Venice Biennale/Space Design of Japanese Pavilion (1995), Stage in the Forest, and Toyoma Center for Performing Arts, for which he received the 1997 Architectural Institute of Japan Annual Award.

Atsushi Kitagawara
architect
MA RA MJIA MAIJ

Atsushi Kitagawara Architects, Inc.
2-6-13 Mita, Minato-ku
Tokyo 108, Japan
TEL 03-5442-1751
FAX 03-5442-1731

株式会社北川原温建築都市研究所代表
日本建築学会会員
日本建築家協会会員
東京芸術大学講師
早稲田大学講師

Atsushi Kitagawara

Kitagawara was born in Nagano, Japan, 1951. As a student at the Tokyo University of Fine Arts, he

Dr. KISHO KUROKAWA
architecte d.p.l.g.
Hon. FAIA Hon. FRIBA

KISHO KUROKAWA architect & associates
66, rue Cortagrelle
75013 Paris France
Tel :33-1-47.72.62.79
Fax:33-1-47.72.58.23

Professor
Tsinghua University, Beijing,
People's Republic of China

KISHO KUROKAWA architect & associates
Aoyama Bldg. 11F
1-2-3 Kita-Aoyama, Minato-ku
Tokyo 107 Japan
Tel : 81-3-3404-3481
Fax : 81-3-3479-5088
Internet : kurokawa @ kisho. co. jp
www home page : http://www.kisho.co.jp

Kisho Kurokawa

1934	Born in Nagoya.
1957	Graduated Kyoto University, Department of Architecture.
1960	One of the founders of the Metabolism movement.
1964	Tokyo University, Doctoral Course, Graduate School of Architecture.

Principal Works

1977	National Ethnological Museum.
1983	National Bunraku Theater.
1987	Nagoya City Art Museum.
1988	Hiroshima City Museum of Contemporary Art.
1989	Japanese-German Center in Berlin, Germany.
1990	Chinese-Japanese Youth Center, China.
1991	Melbourne Central, Australia.
1992	Pacific Tower, France.
1993	Museum of Modern Art, Wakayama.
1994	Ehime Prefectural Museum of General Science.

Awards

1965	Takamura Kotaro Design Award.
Also in	1977, 1978, 1979, 1983, 1989, 1991, 1993 Building Constructors Society Award.
1976	Honorary Fellow of RIBA (first Japanese architect).
1978	Mainichi Art Award.
1979	Madara Bulgarian First Order, Bulgaria.
1981	Honorary Fellow of AIA.
1985	Honorary Professor, University of Buenos Aires, Argentina.
1986	Gold Medal from the Academy of Architecture, France.
1988	Richard Neutra Award from California State Polytechnic University, U.S.A.
1988	Commandeur de l'Ordre du Lion de Finlande, Finland.
1988	Doctor's Degree of Philosophy (Honoris Causa) at Sofia University, Bulgaria.
1989	Chevalier de l'Ordre des Arts et des Lettres from the Ministry of Culture, France.
1989	Grand Prix with Gold Medal at the Fifth World Biennale of Architecture, Sofia, Bulgaria.
1990	Honorary Member of the Union of Architects in Bulgaria
1990	Member of the Ordre des Architectes, France.
1991	Prize of Architectural Institute of Japan.
1992	Prize of Japan Art Academy.
1994	Academician of the International Academy of Architecture.
1995	Honorary Professor, Tongji University, China.
1995	Honorary Professor, Georgian Technical University, Republic of Georgia.
1997	AIA Los Angeles Pacific Rim Award (first awarded).
1998	Doctor's Degree of Humanities (Honoris Causa) at Newport Asia Pacific University, California.

Publications

1965	*Urban Design.*
1969	*Homo Movens.*
1982	*Thesis on Architecture I.*
1987	*Philosophy of Symbiosis.*
1989	*The Era of Nomad.*
1990	*Thesis on Architecture II.*
1991	*Hanasuki.*
1991	*Poems on Architecture.*
1994	*Kisho Kurokawa Note.*

Fumihiko Maki

1928	Born in Tokyo, Japan.
1952	Bachelor of Architecture, University of Tokyo.

FUMIHIKO MAKI	
PRINCIPAL	
MAKI AND ASSOCIATES	
13-4 Hachiyama-cho, Shibuya-ku, Tokyo 150-0035, Japan	
Tel. 03-3780-3880 Fax. 03-3780-3881	

代表取締役

株式会社 槇総合計画事務所
建築・都市設計

槇 文 彦

株式会社 槇総合計画事務所
〒一五〇-〇〇三五
東京都渋谷区鉢山町十三番四号
電話(代)〇三-三七八〇-三八八〇
FAX・〇三-三七八〇-三八八一

1953	Master of Architecture, Cranbrook Academy of Art, U.S.A.
1954	Master of Architecture, Graduate School of Design, Harvard University.
1956–58	Assistant Professor, Washington University.
1958–60	Graham Foundation Fellow.
1960–62	Associate Professor, Washington University.
1962–65	Associate Professor, GSD Harvard University.
1965–85	Visiting Critic at universities in U.S.A. and Europe.
1979–89	Professor, Department of Architecture, University of Tokyo.

Principal Works

1960	Toyota Memorial Hall, Nagoya University.
1967–92	Hillside Terrace Apartment Complex (6 phases), Tokyo.
1972	Prefectural Sports Center, Osaka.
1979	Iwasaki Art Museum, Ibusuki, Kagoshima.
1984	Municipal Gymnasium, Fujisawa, Kanagawa.
1985	SPIRAL, Tokyo.
1986	National Museum of Modern Art, Kyoto.
1989	TEPIA, A Science Pavilion, Tokyo.
1989	Makuhari Messe, Chiba.

1990	Metropolitan Gymnasium, Tokyo.
1991–94	Keio University, Shonan Fujisawa Campus, Kanagawa.
1993	Yerba Buena Gardens, Visual Arts Center, San Francisco.
1993	Isar Biiro Park Hallbergmoos, Munich.
1994	Kirishima International Concert Hall, Kagoshima.
1995	Tokyo Church of Christ, Tokyo.
1996	Kaze-no-Oka Crematorium, Nakatsu, Gita.
1996	Fukuoka University Student Center, Fukuoka.
1997	Natori Performing Arts Center, Miyagi.
1998	Makuhari Messe Phase II, Chiba.

Awards

	Member, Japan Institute of Architects.
	Honorary Fellow, American Institute of Architects.
	Honorary Fellow, Royal Institute of British Architects.
1963	Japan Institute of Architecture for Tokyo Memorial Hall.
1985	Japan Institute of Architecture for Fujisawa Municipal Gymnasium.
1987	Reynolds Memorial Award for SPIRAL.
1988	Wolf Prize, Israel.
1988	Chicago Architecture Award.
1990	Thomas Jefferson Medal in Architecture, University of Virginia.
1993	The Pritzker Architecture Prize.
1993	UIA Gold Medal.
1993	Prince of Wales Prize in Urban Design, Harvard University (for Hillside Terrace).

Publications

1960	*Metabolism 1960.*
1964	*Investigations in Collective Form*, Washington University.
1965	*Movement Systems in the City*, Graduate School of Design, Harvard University.
1965	"Some Thoughts on Collective Form" (co-author), *Structure in Art and Science*, ed. G. Kepes.
1965	Japanese translation of *Communitas* by Paul and Percival Goodman.
1978	*Fumihiko Maki 1: 1965–78, Contemporary Architects Series.*
1979	*Miegakuresuru Toshi: a Morphological Analysis of the City of Edo-Tokyo.*

1986	*Fumihiko Maki 2: 1979–86, Contemporary Architects Series.*
1987	*Design Methodology in Technology and Science,* (co-author).
1989	*Fragmentary Figures: The Collected Architectural Drawings of Fumihiko Maki.*
1992	*Kioku no Keizo: A Collection of Essays.*
1993	*Fumihiko Maki 3: 1986–92, Contemporary Architects Series.*
1997	*Fumihiko Maki, Building and Projects,* Princeton Architectural Press.

1991	Autopolis Art Museum.
1992	Sea-Folk Museum.
1993	House No.14, Tsukuba.
1993	Shima Art Museum.
1997	Ushibuka Fisherman's Wharf.
1997	Chihiro Art Museum, Azumino.
1997	Tenshin Memorial Museum of Art, Ibaraki.

Awards

1993	Education Minister's Art Encouragement Prize for Freshman.
1993	The Prize of Architectural Institute of Japan for Design.
1993	Isoya Yoshida Memorial Prize.

Hiroshi Naito

内藤廣建築設計事務所　　Naito Architect & Associates
東京都千代田区九段南2-2-8　301 Matsuoka-Kudan Bldg.
松岡九段ビル301 〒102-0074　2-2-8 Kudan-Minami, Chiyoda-ku
Tokyo 102-0074 JAPAN

内　藤　　廣

03-3262-9636

Hiroshi Naito

1950	Born in Yokohama.
1974	Waseda University, Tokyo, B.Arch.; won the Murano Award.
1974–76	Studied under Professor Takamasa Yoshizaka at Graduate School of Waseda University.
1976–78	Worked in an Architectural Office of Fernand Higueras in Madrid, Spain, as a Chief Architect.
1979–81	Worked in architectural office of Kiyonori Kikutake (Tokyo).
1981	Established own architectural office, Naito Architect & Associates.
1986–88, 1990–95	Lecturer at Waseda University.

Principal Works

1984	Gallery TOM.
1984	House No.1, Kamakura.

Kazuo Shinohara

1925	Born in Shizuoka Prefecture, Japan.
1953	Degree from the Tokyo Technical University.
1953	Instructor at Tokyo Technical University.
1970	Full professor at Tokyo Technical University.

Principal Works

1961	Umbrella House, Tokyo.
1966	House in White, Tokyo.
1971	Cubical Forest Lodge, Kawasaki.
1976	House in Uehara.
1984	Shinohara House, Yokohama.
1987	Centennial Hall for the Tokyo Institute of Technology.
1990	Police Headquarters, Kumamoto.

Ryoji Suzuki

1944	Born in Tokyo.
1968	Bachelor of Engineering, Department of Architecture, Waseda University.
1968–73	Designing staff of Takenaka Corporation.

1992   Experience in Material N.35 "Clairière, Creux, Vide" (16mm film).

Ryoji Suzuki

1970   Established own firm of architects.
1977   Master of Engineering, Voshiro Ikehara Laboratory, Department of Architecture, Waseda University.
1982   Renamed practice Ryoji Suzuki Architect & Partners.
1997   Professor at Waseda University.

Principal Works

1987   Experience in Material N.20 Azabu Edge.
1988   Experience in Material N.27 Cathedral Chair.
1990   Experience in Material N.32 House in Sagishima.
1991   Experience in Material N.33 Kohunji Temple.
1997   Experience in Material N.37 Project in Sagishima (Prize for Architectural Institute of Japan).
1998   Experience in Material N.38 Ashikita Youth Center.

Awards

1990   Second Prize for the Japanese Cultural Center in Paris Competition.
1995   Second Prize for the Yokohama International Port Terminal Design Competition.

Publications

1988   *Architecture in Drawings, Space & Concept: Several Experiences in Material* (Dohosha).
1988   *Dir-Architectural Considerations* (Chikuma).

Riken Yamamoto

1968   Graduated from the school of architecture at Nihon University.
1971   Completed the master course at the school of architecture Tokyo National University of Fine Art and Music.
1971–73   Studied as research student in Dr. Hiroshi Hara's Laboratory at Institute of Industrial Science, University of Tokyo.
1973   Established Riken Yamamoto and Field Shop.
1997   Instructor at Yokohama National University. Instructor at Nihon University.
        Instructor at Tokyo University.
        Instructor at Tokyo Metropolitan University.

Principal Works

1986   Gazebo.
1987   Rotunda.
1987   Hamlet.
1991   Kumamoto Public Housing.
1991   House at Okayama.
1991   Sugita House.
1992–94   Complex of Buildings at Ryokuen-Toshi station.
1996   Iwadeyama Junior High School.
1996   Yamamoto Psychiatric Clinic.
1997   Yokohama Community Center.

Awards

1985 Kajima Award. (SD. Review, 1985).
1988 Architectural Institute of Japan Award, (for Gazebo and Rotunda).
1990 Honorable Mention, international competition for Maison de la Culture du Japon, Paris, France.
1993 1st Prize in the competition for Iwadeyama Junior High School.
1994 Architecture of the Year (for Xystus).
1995 2nd Prize, international competition for Yokohama Ferry Port Terminal.
      1st Prize, competition for Saitama Prefectural University of Nursing and Welfare.
1996 1st Prize, competition for Hiroshima Nishi Fire Station.
1997 1st Prize, competition for Hakodate Municipal College.
1998 Mainichi Art Awards for Iwadeyama Junior High School.

HAJIME YATSUKA
PRESIDENT
ARCHITECTS PLANNING OFFICE

UPM CO., LTD.
401 SHANPOLE-HIGASHIMATSUBARA   TEL : (03)3321-9925
5-56-10 MATSUBARA SETAGAYA-KU TOKYO 156 JAPAN   FAX : (03)3321-9935

株式会社ユーピーエム 一級建築士事務所
東京都世田谷区松原5-56-10 シャンポール東松原401
TEL (03)3321-9925 FAX (03)3321-9935 〒156

代表取締役

八束 はじめ
HAJIME YATSUKA

Hajime Yatsuka

1948 Born in Yamagata City, Japan.
1973 Graduated from Tokyo University Tutors: Kenzo Tange and Sachio Otani, then a student of the graduate course.
1979 Retired from Tokyo University Atelier Arata. Worked on such projects as Tsukuba Center Building, Museum of Contemporary Art (Los Angeles).

1984 Left Isozaki's office, established own firm, UPM.

Principal Works

1984 Okabe House (realized; Tokyo).
      Synaps project (non-realized; Tokyo).
      Komagane Cultural Complex (competition; Komagane).
1985 Sotokawa Beauty Shop (realized; Kyoto).
1986 Shonandai Cultural Complex (competition; Fujisawa).
1987 Angelo Tarlazzi House (boutique, realized; Tokyo).
      House in Kajigaya (realized; Tokyo).
1988 House in Komae (realized; Tokyo).
1989 Media Luna (building of mixed use, realized; Kobe).
      K2 Oyamadai (shops, realized; Tokyo).
      Cikawa clinic (clinic and residence, realized; Hadano).
1990 Takeyasu clinic (clinic and residence, realized; Yokohama).
      Folly 12 & 13, EXPO 90 (realized; Osaka).
      OMY building (office, project; Omiya).
      Nobby (car gallery, project; Hadano).
      Sports hall for Bunkyo University (in progress; Koshigaya).
1991 The Wing (commercial building, realized; Nishinomiya).
      House in Hayama (residence, project; Hayama).
1992 Triadic Tower (Urban complex, project; Sakai).
      Nasunogahara Harmony Hall (auditorium, competition; Nasunogahara).
      Nara Convention Hall (auditorium, competition; Nara).
1993 Center House of Bunkyo University (in progress; Koshigaya).
      Niigata Civic Center (auditorium, competition, 2nd prize; Niigata).
1994 Tokyo GEIMU Headquarters (office, realized; Tokyo).
      Tohoku Historical Museum (competition; Tagajo).
      Aya-uta Cultural Hall (auditorium / project; Aya-uta).
      Mattoh City Hall (project; Mattoh).

1995   Yokohama Ferry terminal
        (competition; Yokohama).
        Sendai Médiatèque
        (competition; Sendai).
        Gymnasium, Bunkyo University
        (realized; Koshigaya).
1996   Center for Multi-Media
        (under construction; Shiroisi).

1997   Center House, Bunkyo University
        (realized; Koshigaya).
1998   School of Human Science,
        Bunkyo University (realized;
        Koshigaya).
        Folly in the Echigo Hillside
        National Government Park
        (realized; Nagaoka).

Photographic
Acknowledgments

All photographs are by Christopher Knabe and
Joerg Rainer Noennig unless otherwise stated.

Front cover: © R. Suzuki.
pp. 14, 15: © Wilhelm Klauser.
p. 30, left: © Shinkenchiku-Sha;
      top right: © Shigeru Ohno;
      bottom right: © Shigeru Ohno.
p. 47, all photos: © R. Suzuki.
p. 49: © R. Suzuki.
p. 52, all photos: © R. Suzuki.
p. 53: © Shigeo Anzai.
p. 64, bottom: © Shigeru Ohno.
p. 67: © Shigeru Ohno.
p. 74, all photos: © T. Ogawa.
p. 89, top: © Mitsumasa Fujitsuka.
p. 92, all photos: © Christopher Knabe.
p. 93, center: © Tomio Ohashi.
p. 95, all photos: © Naoya Hatakeyama.
p. 96, all photos: © Naoya Hatakeyama.
p. 98, top and bottom: © Naoya Hatakeyama.
p. 108: © Eiichiro Sakata.
p. 111, bottom: © Yasuhiro Ishimoto.
p. 113, top: © Yasuhiro Ishimoto.
p. 116: © Fujitsuka Mitsumasa.
p. 128: © Fujitsuka Mitsumasa.
p. 130, all photos: © Fujitsuka Mitsumasa.
p. 133: © Fujitsuka Mitsumasa.
p. 138: © Tomio Ohashi.
p. 139: © Yoshikatsu Saeki.
p. 141: © Osamu Mirai.
p. 144: © Koji Taki.
p. 145: © Tomio Ohashi.
p. 146: © Tomio Ohashi.
Back cover, left: © T. Ogawa.